THE ECONOMICS OF LIBIDO

THE ECONOMICS OF LIBIDO

Psychic Bisexuality, the Superego, and the Centrality of the Oedipus Complex

Trevor C. Pederson

KARNAC

First published in 2015 by
Karnac Books Ltd
118 Finchley Road
London NW3 5HT

British Library Cataloguing in Publication Data

A C.I.P. for this book is available from the British Library

ISBN-13: 978-1-78220-177-9

Typeset by V Publishing Solutions Pvt Ltd., Chennai, India

www.karnacbooks.com

CONTENTS

ABOUT THE AUTHOR

Trevor Pederson is a mental health counsellor and psychoanalyst in private practice in Casper, Wyoming. He is a doctoral candidate at the Boston Graduate School of Psychoanalysis. His dissertation introduces a methodology for the psychoanalytic interpretation of film.

PREFACE

I came to psychoanalysis from philosophy. I was interested in synthesising the work of Marx and Nietzsche and along the way I came across references to Freud and Wilhelm Reich. I came to see that Reich had already successfully combined their work together, although it had only been in spirit and not in letter. Not too long after I came across the work of Lacan and Žižek and became enamoured with it for a time. If Reich had been the spirit then Lacan surely was the letter of what the change was to be. At least, the contradictions in their thought didn't bother me too much at first. They existed side by side until I entered a counselling programme and began the slow process of looking for ways to communicate the experience of sitting with a patient. Faced with this challenge it was the work of Reich and his characterology that allowed me to gain a foothold. The broad designation of obsessional and hysteric was favoured by a few of my classmates and one or two even attempted to make use of masculine *vs.* feminine jouissance but there were no clear definitions of these concepts. More often than not it appeared that anatomical sex alone was the justification for labelling others. During this process I found myself forced to read a lot of Freud. I didn't like it. I believed, as many do now, that the present always represents some progress and that Freud's predecessors must represent an advance. Strangely, I didn't feel this way at all about philosophy. Whenever I read Heidegger, Sartre, or any of the twentieth century philosophers I always thought that they were a backsliding from the height that Nietzsche and Marx represented. Soon I came to realise that Freud also possessed a rigour that psychoanalysis had fallen from and that in the framework of classical psychoanalysis belonged the examples, the psychodynamics, and the arguments that allowed concepts to be operationalised.

As I was studying Freud I found myself defending him against all those who remained "presentists" and judged him as necessarily being a product of his time and lacking when compared with contemporary theorists. The designation of hysteria was the first battleground. I had read cases of passive men, masochistic men, and men with hysteria so I knew I couldn't be satisfied with sex alone in assessing any problems. However, as I began to look into the literature I was troubled to see that there were several articles pointing to the fact that a conversion symptom alone is not enough to determine hysteria and that they are sometimes found with obsessive compulsive disorder (OCD) in the same individual. Additionally, there were definitions of hysteria that didn't have anything to do with symptoms and related to what the The Diagnostic and Statistical Manual of Mental Disorders (DSM) classified as histrionic personality disorder. This disorder seemed to have nothing to do with the classic psychoanalytic definition of being disgusted with sex or taking revenge against, or hating, men (as found in the female castration complex). However, Reich's hysteric had a lot in common with the histrionic personality disorder, and the judgmental type of hysteric who was resentful towards men and felt above sex was aligned with the female compulsive character. I continued to research Freud's active and passive designation and to search the literature on hysteria and this eventually led me to the first chapter of this book on psychic bisexuality and its application to hysterical character.

I found that the more I read Freud, the more that references to Lacan dropped away in my work. Either he was, as he claimed, a dutiful student of Freud and his ideas were subsumed under Freud's original designations, or Lacan's lack of clinical or phenomenological examples didn't allow his concepts any traction in the clinic. Many Lacanians I have met criticise "outsiders" who only want to talk about the mirror phase but this is one of the only concepts of his that is a coherent claim and, ironically, it doesn't hold up when studied against childhood development. So, although I initially accepted the Lacanian criticism against ego psychology as the ideologically influenced and cowardly version of psychoanalysis, I began to appreciate it more because the writers actually gave examples and made arguments based upon them. Edith Jacobson and Annie Reich were doing much, much more than referencing the rational decision-making that entered after the Oedipus complex and their work on the ego ideal intrigued me.

It was during this period that I found the work of Chasseguet-Smirgel. It wasn't until I read her that I understood the significance of the Oedipus complex in both its active and passive forms. In earlier work I had seen the importance of the ego ideal in the succession of father-substitutes but her examples of perversion and the regression of the ego ideal made me think in a completely different way. Returning to Freud's texts with new eyes, I followed the threads and found that conscience required a further stage of development, the father complex, which seemed to have been completely ignored in the literature. Moreover, the tiny step between the Oedipus complex and father complex included much that could revitalise that connection of psychoanalysis with other academic disciplines. As for the regressive ego ideal, for a long time I stumbled, as I believe Chasseguet-Smirgel did, with what appeared to be the mistake of attributing too much cognition to the child. This was where my fullest appreciation of Freud emerged and the insight of his Copernican revolution. After this point I found the many other analyst that appear in the book when I was researching specific concepts.

Along with this brief acknowledgement of the writers that contributed to the development of my approach to psychoanalysis, I have to acknowledge some other individuals. I'd like to thank Arielle Zibrak, my partner, for the love and support she's given. I'd also like to thank her family for their graciousness, especially her father, Dr. Joseph Zibrak. I'd like to thank my family, especially my grandparents, and also Lindy Dowhaniuk who has a place there. I've benefitted from conversations and walks with Michael Williams and Fabiana Vasconcelos. I'd like to thank Dr. John Madonna and Dr. Richard Kradin for analysis. I'd like to thank Michael Eigen for being encouraging when I needed support and also Dr. Edward Weisband for reaching out to me. I need to thank Dr. Thomas Twyman for letting me have freedom in research and Dr. Max Cavallaro for his feedback on the essay that became the second chapter. Lastly, I'd like to thank Nico, for his energy and affection.

INTRODUCTION

In the work that follows I lay out three shibboleths of psychoanalysis: psychic bisexuality, the Oedipus complex, and social ontology. I'm sure that some would dispute the first while most probably have no idea what the third is. If you dispute the second, then I'm not sure why you would bother to call yourself a psychoanalyst these days unless you were a masochist or the name managed to retain some tone of reverence in one's family—it certainly doesn't in universities. However, if one recognises Oedipus as a shibboleth then Freud clearly states the importance of bisexuality:

> closer study usually discloses the more complete Oedipus complex, which is twofold, positive and negative, and is due to the bisexuality originally present in children: that is to say, a boy has not merely an ambivalent attitude towards his father and an affectionate object-choice towards his mother, but at the same time he also behaves like a girl and displays an affectionate feminine attitude to his father and a corresponding jealousy and hostility towards his mother. It is this complicating element introduced by bisexuality that makes it so difficult to obtain a clear view of the facts in connection with the earliest object-choices and

identifications, and still more difficult to describe them intelligibly. (Freud, 1923b, p. 33)

Even in Freud's late work on female sexuality he explicitly recognises different types of triangulation that are subsumed under the term Oedipus complex which he holds "to include all the child's relations to *both* parents" or triangular relationships in general (Freud, 1931a, p. 226, emphasis mine). Although the castration complex is sometimes used synonymously with the Oedipus complex, I have found it valuable to separate them based upon Freud's use of the superego in structural theory. Since the superego is the heir of the Oedipus complex, or creates a paternal imago that allows for a father-substitute to be put into the ego ideal, then the Oedipus complex denotes that which causes the individual to reject the father-substitute, choose to be his own father, disregard the incest-taboo, and, in doing so, experience the castration complex. This is not wholly idiosyncratic because Freud (1914b, 1937) himself identifies the castration complex with Adler's masculine protest and the rejection of the father-substitute. Moreover, the actual myth of Oedipus begins with the father abandoning the child and then the father dying without any triangulation involving the mother. The true triangle begins afterwards with the blind seer Tiresias as the third who threatens the happiness of Oedipus and his mother and, ultimately ends with, Oedipus blinding himself in identification with him.

Ontology is a term that arises from philosophy that is defined as the study of being. Social ontology, as I use it here, refers to the intersubjectivity of the primary identification that forms the paternal imago not just at the Oedipus complex but throughout development. An individual doesn't only experience the castration complex and the rejection of the father's authority in analysis but with teachers, bosses, and other superiors. The father imago is a constant relation, and there is much evidence that Freud considered there to be multiple identifications with the parents throughout development and therefore multiple superego relations. Freud writes:

> nor must it be forgotten that a child has a different estimate of its parents at different periods of its life. At the time at which the Oedipus complex gives place to the super-ego they are something quite magnificent; but later they lose much of this. Identifications then come about with these later parents as well, and indeed

they regularly make important contributions to the formation of character; *but in that case they only* affect *the ego, they no longer influence the* super-ego, *which has been determined by the earliest parental imagos.* (Freud, 1933, p. 64, emphasis mine)

Freud's language is unequivocal here: the child's estimates of its parents' perfection determines the superego by primary identifications with the parents that leave their traces in imagos. The enormous world of "thing-presentations", as opposed to the much later world of the sign or "word presentation", opens up. Freud sees the superego as connected to the earliest narcissism of the child and the question becomes how can the pre-sign child conceive of the different forms of perfection and power that he estimates the parents to have and is then demanded to follow himself after their internalisation? So, either Freud, as Klein is often charged with, holds that the child is capable of understanding complex relations of power back to the early oral phase of identification with the father, or a reversal of priority must take place (Freud, 1933, p. 63). By this I mean that instead of considering the child atomistically and needing to appeal to its cognitive faculties we consider the child as primarily related to the object—as a social animal. The parents' perfection then becomes part of "the transitional space" between the child and parent and takes on a negative existence. The question is not "what are the reasons the atomistic individual has to be social?" but, rather, "what defence is operating if the person isn't searching for recognition, love, or approval?"

This reversal is the fundamental insight of the ego drive in psychoanalysis. The ambitious person isn't someone who has rationally chosen the value of being successful. The ambitious person is "driven" to be successful and will suffer inferiority, or jealousy if he isn't admired by others as successful or having the potential to be. This constitutes the Copernican revolution in psychoanalysis. Freud (1930) holds that anything that we'd identify as striving for happiness is a matter of the drive-based or psychical constitution (pp. 83–84). It is this claim that gives us the horizon of the castration complex. In contrast, the post-oedipal father complex isn't about individual happiness but establishes the first post-ambivalent tie to culture. Narcissistic triumph is transmuted into sharing the reference point of commitment in marriage and fairness with others in one's community. In the following latency superego the move from individual narcissism to social narcissism is completed as one shares the common ideal of a "group mind" in race, class, and creed (Freud, 1921, p. 129).

The active, or what I'll identify as the egoistic person, doesn't want to be "driven". He or she wants to feel in control. To be driven is a blow to the egoist's narcissism or self-esteem and therefore the ego drives are only to be regarded as partial—ones of exhibition or scopophilia—or the superego can only exist post-oedipally and consist of linguistically mediated values that are chosen. However, as psychoanalysis continues to die out in universities, and its former glory now invites mockery and derision, it is beginning to attract more of the passive, or what I'll identify as altruistic people. These people don't require the same illusion of control that the egoists do and their hunger is for the communication of their experience of others. This book is an attempt to give psychoanalysis over to them—if they can find the courage to stand up and take it. For this will mean that they may have to overcome their feeling of inadequacy with theory, fears of being seen as presumptuous or "stealing the spotlight" from teachers who were taught different models, and tolerate the anger of other egoists who must be in control. My hope is that their drives to give and help, or to be unique and interesting, carry them through these feelings.

* * *

This book is a return to Freud *qua* psychologist in order to affirm the centrality of the Oedipus complex, understand the contributions of the drives to gender, and illustrate the characterological functioning of the pre-phallic superego. This book is also an attempt to begin the work of synthesising the different schools of psychoanalysis into a unified theory. To be sure, there is much work left to do and this book is a sketch, an opening salvo, and thus an invitation for others to bring their blood. It's a counter pressure to the trend to place too much emphasis on linguistically mediated values. It's the replacement of God with the ancestor and asking the Adlerian, the neo-Freudian, the Kleinian, the Kohutian, and other schools to look for their family resemblance instead of their own perfection.

The central argument I make in the text, under the heading of social ontology, is that Freud gives a model of the personality that is built upon the primary relatedness of the individual through the drives. An individual doesn't rationally choose to be ambitious, shy, arrogant, or kind based upon values but, rather, these are part of his "psychical constitution" of ego and object drives and their relation to the superego. The importance of this can be understood by the implication that, all things being equal, much of political behaviour can be understood as issuing from the emphasis of active-egoistic (Republican) or passive-altruistic (Democrat) drives in the individual.

In the first chapter I examine the passive and active in psychoanalysis in Freud's concept of psychic bisexuality. Here I examine Freud's psychological remarks to translate his generic terms into common language and, in doing so, I seek to corroborate his views with the work of other major analysts. Ultimately, I argue that activity and passivity basically stand for egoism and altruism and that they are different than masculine and feminine which have their own form in each pole. Along the egoistic pole I point out that someone can be narcissistic or possess an attitude of superiority (arrogance, vanity) about their physical or intellectual potency (subject egoism) as well as about their beauty, aesthetic refinements, or judgement of the lack of virtues in others (object egoism). Additionally, I point out that someone can masochistically put the desires of others before her own (subject altruism) or masochistically desire the approval of others or have the need to be liked or be seen as interesting by others (object altruism). The former is tied to "people-pleasing", being "self-effacing" etc. and the latter is tied to being a "people person", endearing, and wanting to be the centre of attention, not for the admiration of one's skills or potency, but to share enthusiasm, or to be interesting.

In the second chapter I use David Milrod, as a recent exponent of ego psychology, to criticise the popular understanding of the Oedipus complex and superego and show several major misinterpretations of Freud's work. I show that Freud identified the subsequent "father complex" as the point at which the guilt conscience arises and not the Oedipus complex. Moreover, this guilt conscience isn't based upon linguistically mediated values for Freud but draws its strength against aggressive actions due to prohibition from a parental imago (or internalisation of the parent). Ultimately, I argue that the centrality of the Oedipus complex is that it is a modification of the ego and object drives so that the individual recognises "father-substitutes" who are granted a transference of having more skill or knowledge than one. Thus, a high school diploma, BA, MA, doctorate, etc. broadly represent "maturation" and interactions with father-substitutes, as can someone who makes more money or has membership to different prestigious clubs. Any culture that recognises the difference between neophytes and elders with more knowledge or skill (or magic) demonstrates the existence of the Oedipus complex. However, the castration complex, in which one gets into rivalries with father-substitutes and fears their wrath or punishment, doesn't exist in every culture. Lastly, I show, *contra* ego psychologists, that the superego has both pre-phallic forms and continues developing into latency. The later developments have important implications for political behaviour and I show the implications that this more nuanced view has for clinicians as well as connections that can be made with sociology, gender studies, and the understanding of ideology.

In the third chapter, I examine two ways in which the pre-oedipal superego reveals itself in character. The first is by linking Freud's work to the transcendental idealism of the philosopher Kant. The second is by examining the depth structures of egoism and altruism in the negative existence of perfection and death. Contra ego psychologists, Lacanians, self-psychologists, etc. who place the bulk of navigating the world on sophisticated cognition and linguistically mediated values, and relegate the pre-oedipal to phantasy involved in pathology, I show that classical psychoanalysis is justified in many of its insights. By placing primacy on social, instead of individual, ontology, Freud anchors seemingly complex concepts not in individual understanding but in the relationship to parental imagos. I argue that Freud and other classical analysts provide the foundation for four different levels of Being that correspond to the auto-erotic, the narcissistic, the anal, and the phallic stage. They in turn correspond with the subjective encounter with Space, Time, the Superlative, and Prestige and are rooted in Freud's conception of negativity underpinning the transference and sense of perfection or death in the parents. I use epic films such as *Star Wars* to illustrate how drives can interact with father-substitutes. For example, Darth Vader is portrayed as more skilled and powerful than Luke (phallic) and the Emperor who rules the galaxy is seen as the most powerful or closest to omniscience (anal). Obi-Wan and Yoda are beings outside of the social hierarchies of power and the magic/psychic abilities that they, and other characters, possess in "the force" reflect a power that defies Time in the sense that such power does not exist and gives more credence to wishes than the investigation of the efficacy of wishes over time. Lastly, the creation of a new fantasy world that rivals our world is the displacement of the father-substitute of Space.

The last section is an appendix that provides Wittgenstein's private language argument. I've included it because it gives justification for the phenomenological/common language approach I use in order to establish psychic bisexuality and it allows me to pre-empt a lot of criticism my approach will receive. Wittgenstein's private language argument on one hand, shows that standard arguments for humanity's rational nature from things like mathematics don't actually work. On the other hand, it shows that sensation, emotional, and motivational language can't arise from introspection and must arise from EQ or judgement of the behaviour and actions of others that can be shared among experts. I broadly separate views that don't recognise a dialectic between the inputs of individual personality and culture into three errors: mechanistic, relativistic, and mystical. This is based upon whether they ignore the value of consciousness in understanding motivations, place motivation solely in cultural determination, or claim an atomistic rational essence and will (respectively).

CHAPTER ONE

Psychic bisexuality

In Freud's late phase he offers us a view of the economy of libido based upon an individual's characterological or drive-based constitution. He writes:

> happiness, in the reduced sense in which we recognize it as possible, is a problem of the *economics of the individual's libido*. There is no golden rule which applies to everyone: every man must find out for himself in what particular fashion he can be saved. All kinds of different factors will operate to direct his choice. It is a question of how much real satisfaction he can expect to get from the external world, how far he is led to make himself independent of it, and, finally, how much strength he feels he has for altering the world to suit his wishes. In this, *his psychical constitution will play a decisive part, irrespectively of the external circumstances*. The man who is predominantly erotic will give first preference to his emotional relationships to other people; the narcissistic man, who inclines to be self-sufficient, will seek his main satisfactions in his internal mental processes; the man of action will never give up the external world on which he can try out his strength ... success is never certain, for that depends on the convergence of many factors, perhaps on

1

> none more than on the *capacity of the psychical constitution to adapt its function to the environment* and then to exploit that environment for a yield of pleasure. A person who is born with a specially unfavourable *instinctual constitution*, and who has not properly undergone the transformation and rearrangement of his libidinal components which is indispensable for later achievements, will find it hard to obtain happiness from his external situation, especially if he is faced with tasks of some difficulty. (Freud, 1930, pp. 83–84, emphasis mine)

In this quotation Freud is drawing our attention to the fact that people have characteristic ways of approaching the world and that a person can't simply change his way. You can't tell someone whose "economy of libido" is built around finding romantic love that he should stop wasting time and focus on advancing in his career and that he'll find love after he achieves some success. The nights of studying and working alone aren't backed up by anticipatory feelings of power or the ability to imagine the admiration or jealousy of others. Such a person doesn't find satisfaction in competing with peers; rather, he is driven to find someone whom he can idealise, find his happiness in making his significant other happy, and feel his self-worth by being loved in return. Similarly, the ambitious person isn't free to simply choose to base his life around love. He experiences jealousy when peers receive a better position, make more money, have a more attractive sexual partner than him, or when his possession of these things is threatened by someone who he feels is more potent.

I must confess that I don't understand the post-modernists who say that we can never understand people from different cultures and historical eras. Whether I read Plato, Shakespeare, Dostoevsky, or authors of today the same strivings for different types of happiness are there and the same types of character structures populate their works. The ambitious person may compete with others to be the best warrior in one culture and be jealous of another man's corner office in another, but the social relations are the same. An ambitious person will find the content of his ambition given by his historically determined political-economy and even if cultural values encourage competition among all people of that culture, he will still be driven to go beyond what is the norm. Feelings of jealousy and an economic emphasis on self-consciousness in regard to his "image" will set him apart from others. Moreover, if one speaks of French, German, etc. "character" there are always many people in the population who aren't artistic romantics or punctual and businesslike, or whatever the stereotype may be.

As it stands, there is still an incredible amount of content that has to be understood in psychoanalytic characterology. What is ego drive, ego ideal, and how different forms of striving for "perfection" are to be conceived of is unclear in the literature. Moreover, the determinants of economic significance such as fixation, adaptation, partial or full identifications, etc. have yet to be clearly conceptualised. In this chapter I won't be performing this work. Instead, I will attempt to stake some phenomenological coordinates that I hope will contribute to a larger undertaking. This chapter was initially born of the desire to understand hysterical character, given all the different definitions and motivations ascribed to this personality type. Between the wealth of insight that some analysts give the impression of hoarding in their private practice, and the poverty of conceptual clarity in the public sphere, I've returned to Freud to find a way out. The Freud I've returned to is the one who asks us to stick to common language and the motivations, desires, and feelings found there in order to understand others:

> in ego-psychology it will be difficult to escape from what is universally known; it will rather be a question of new ways of looking at things and new ways of arranging them than of new discoveries. (Freud, 1933, p. 60)
>
> We call this organization their "ego." Now there is nothing new in this. Each one of us makes this assumption without being a philosopher ... In psycho-analysis we like to keep in contact with the popular mode of thinking and prefer to make its concepts scientifically serviceable rather than reject them. (Freud, 1926b, p. 195)

After sharing my investigation into psychic bisexuality and the ego and object drives in Freud's work, I will attempt to elaborate on these concepts with the work of other analysts. My aim is to establish a general consensus between analysts across two poles: a competitive and self-idealising pole that is "active-egoistic", and a restorative and other-idealising pole that is "passive-altruistic". After investigating some of Freud's concerns about psychic bisexuality I suggest that he doesn't displace its centrality by using the terms active and passive but, rather, is struggling for a more sophisticated definition. Returning to scattered remarks in his texts and those of early analysts, I argue that the active-passive binary is something separate from the masculine and feminine binary and suggests that there is a masculine and feminine position along both poles. Ultimately, I argue that this creates four basic *libidinal positions*. Along the competitive and self-idealising pole there is a subject-masculine position that competes in relation to skill or knowledge and an object-feminine position that competes with others to be the object of desire to a powerful subject. Along the restorative and other-idealising pole there is a subject-feminine position that restores outsiders so they can enjoy belonging, and an object-masculine position that relates to others by being the object of delight to a loving subject. After formalising these four positions I briefly illustrate their usefulness by differentiating between the object egoistic and object altruistic forms of hysteria that several analysts have described.

I

Freud has always emphasised the importance of bisexuality from the beginning of psychoanalysis to his last writings. In the *Three Essays* he writes

> in every normal male or female individual, traces are found of the apparatus of the opposite sex. These either persist without function as rudimentary organs or become modified and take on other functions. These long-familiar facts of anatomy lead us to suppose that an originally bisexual physical disposition has, in the course of evolution, become modified into a unisexual one, leaving behind only a few traces of the sex that has become atrophied. (Freud, 1905b, p. 141)
>
> In human beings pure masculinity or femininity is not to be found either in a psychological or a biological sense. Every individual on the contrary displays a mixture of the character-traits belonging to his own and to the opposite sex; and he shows a combination of activity and passivity whether or not these last character-traits tally with his biological ones. (ibid., p. 219 footnote)

However, by his later writings, Freud lost the confidence to determine what mental, or psychic masculinity and femininity consist of, compared to his earlier writings (Freud, 1905b, p. 144). Although he maintained its importance it became a generic formula:

> we are accustomed to say that every human being displays both male and female instinctual impulses, needs and attributes; but though anatomy, it is true, can point out the characteristic of maleness and femaleness, psychology cannot. For psychology the contrast between the sexes fades away into one between activity and passivity ... (Freud, 1930, p. 105)

Freud's use of activity and passivity isn't simply one of expending a lot of energy in action *vs.* waiting for someone else to do so. Rather, he holds:

> people speak of "active" and "passive" instincts, but it would be more correct to speak of instincts with active and passive aims: for an expenditure of activity is needed to achieve a passive aim as well ... to achieve a passive aim may call for a large amount of activity. (Freud, 1933, p. 96, 115)

Regarding the active and passive, Freud contrasts "two sets of emotional impulses ... opposed to each other ... impulses of an affectionate and submissive nature, but also hostile and defiant ones ..." that align with "fear of castration and desire for castration" (Freud, 1923a, p. 85, 92). The two poles "are completely ambivalent, both affectionate and of a hostile and aggressive nature" and Freud records that the former came to light because its impulses can also be "changed into anxiety ideas" (Freud, 1933, p. 120). In the language of the ego ideal, which "demands perfection", the active pole compels the individual to be perfect and compete with others and the passive pole compels the individual to devote himself to the perfection of the other and seek affection or approval (Freud, 1933, pp. 64–65; 1926a, p. 143). I'm not going to tackle the anxiety associated with the desire for castration or examine the ego ideal further in this chapter. This would both require an intricate study of structural theory and take us away from plain language at the heart of the phenomenological study I proposed. Suffice it to say that Freud's position on the "complete Oedipus complex", which has both active and passive relations to the parents, issues from psychic bisexuality and that understanding its phenomenology provides the first step in establishing formalised triangular complexes (Freud, 1923b, p. 33). I will keep my focus on the surface and make use of another passage in which Freud (1917b) relates the ambivalence of the two poles to egoism and altruism, because altruism best captures the sense of how one can expend a lot of energy that, in contrast to egoism, isn't for personal power or gain (pp. 417–418).

For Freud, egoism concerns the "preservation, assertion, and magnification of the individual" (Freud, 1933, p. 96). In other places he explicitly ties it to Adler's "will to power" (Freud, 1917a, p. 137; 1924b, p. 163). Since egoism is not just the preservation but the "magnification", or will to power of the individual it seems to me that the egoist must go beyond his equal share and conquer what belongs to others or to nature. While food may not always be scarce having the status of being the first in one's field or having the most attractive sexual partner is always scarce. Thus, the active pole can better be defined in relation to the impulses to compete and *to conquer*.

Altruism, as the passive ego drive, can be defined by Freud's concept of eros—before he later paired it with the death drive—as ultimately based upon "love for parents and children, friendship and love for humanity in general, and also devotion to concrete objects and to abstract ideas" (Freud, 1921, p. 90). Instead of conquering, this pole—*to love*—directs the individual to raise up, or restore, the other who is down, or outside of the group, and establish harmony and enjoy "oneness" with them if they are a part of the group or happy (Freud, 1930, p. 66). Again, I want to stick to the surface and don't want to get involved in either a metaphysical debate about altruism requiring complete selfless sacrifice, nor a debate on whether it is merely egoism experienced through a proxy. I want to stick to common language to say that compassion and sympathy are motivations that can be properly ascribed to individuals and doing nice or kind things for, or sharing one's enthusiasm with, friends, family, or others in general can be grant self-esteem. There is a solicitous aspect to know others are well, have their approval, and to elicit stories in order to "vicariously" enjoy their social or sexual adventures. There are no doubt instances of a parent, for example, enjoying the success of her child as egoism through a proxy but the general attitude towards others is my concern here. In common language we can contrast altruism as affable, genial, friendly, amiable, kind, gentle, good natured, good humoured, or warm with egoism as serious, stern, austere, steely, hard, formal, disciplined, having a commanding presence, an authoritative presence, or cool.

At this point a problem might already be salient for my reader. If the active-egoistic and passive-altruistic attitudes are extended to object drives, then this is at odds with Freud positing that anaclitic object choice or idealisation of the beloved is more of a masculine trait than a feminine one (Freud, 1914b, p. 88). However, it must be remembered that Freud (1917b) sees anaclitic love as the culmination of active-egoistic development at the phallic-Oedipus complex resulting from the aim-inhibited impulses towards the mother (p. 417). Before this Freud remarks on "sensual love" that is extinguished after sexual contact, and hate being earlier than love (Freud, 1921, p. 111; 1920, p. 53). It is the height of the active and passive positions in their phallic drive manifestations that concerns me in this chapter.

While hate classically plays a part in pathology like "Don Juan" characters in which "having" the object and moving on to the next is a form of revenge upon women, I'm wary of saying that what is constitutive of the pathological is also part of the norm. Instead, I'd like to follow Freud's discussion of jealousy as a normal part of the relation to the object (Freud, 1922). While unconscious hate may or may not play a part, the emphasis on jealousy concerns whether or not one controls the mental attention of the object so that one is regarded as the potent object. As Freud highlights, jealousy can occur even though the sexual object doesn't cheat, but is merely seen to admire another man. In parallel, "fascination" or "bondage" to the object is a pathology seen in the passive-altruistic object drives, while seeking to erase the boundary between the beloved and oneself is seen as a normal part of love (Freud, 1917b, pp. 417–418; 1930, p. 66). In regard to the former, Freud holds that there is a quality of wanting to get rid of the ego that I understand as an inability to be on one's own. Although, ideas of foppish romantics come to mind, I think that the philosopher Nietzsche gives a more mundane and applicable example that illustrates the masochistic tendency to get rid of the ego:

> I see in many men an excessive impulse and delight in wanting to be a function; they strive after it, and have the keenest scent for all those positions in which precisely they themselves can be functions. Among such persons are those women who transform

themselves into just that function of a man that is but weakly developed in him, and then become his purse, or his politics, or his social intercourse. Such beings maintain themselves best when they insert them selves in an alien organism; if they do not succeed they become vexed, irritated, and eat themselves up. (Nietzsche, 1974, p. 176)

In Nietzsche's example we might describe such an individual as meek or self-effacing or speak of his masochistic drives to devote himself to the perfection of the object. However, again, I'm wary of saying that this pathological behaviour defines the norm. Instead, I want to notice the qualitative distinction between masochistic impulses to devote one-self to the perfection of the other and the desire to merge or resonate with the other. While two egoists might have infamous battles in trying to control each other in order to curb their jealous feelings, Nietzsche articulates the prospective comedy in altruistic love very well:

love wants to spare the person to whom it dedicates itself every feeling of being other, and consequently it is full of dissimulation and pretense of similarity, it is constantly deceiving and feigning a sameness which in reality does not exist. And this happens so instinctively that women in love deny this dissimulation and con-tinual tender deceit and boldly assert that love makes the same (that is to say, that it performs a miracle!).—This process is simple when one party lets himself be loved and does not find it necessary to dissimulate but leave that to the other, loving party; but there is no more confused or impenetrable spectacle than that which arises when both parties are passionately in love with one another and both consequently abandon themselves and want to be the same as one another … (Nietzsche, 1997, p. 210)

Nietzsche's formulation finds the same urge to oneness in love and rec-ognises that both men and women can possess it so that both might remain vague about their desires, in order to share the other's, and that this can create a comedy of errors. This finding is echoed in Freud when he writes that "in women who have had many experiences in love there seems to be no difficulty in finding vestiges of their object-cathexes in the traits of their character" (Freud, 1923b, p. 29). In a person who seeks to control the sexual object and experiences jealousy, one doesn't find that he had become interested in the different kinds of music, hobbies, etc. of those he dated as one would find with the person who idealises the sexual object beyond sensual infatuation. This division is also intimated by Freud when he writes that love and hate belong to different instincts rather than hate coming from frustrated love (Freud, 1920, pp. 53–54). With the altruist, the object drive is best characterised as the drive to merge or resonate with another, and frustrations from the beloved would be followed by reactions of aloneness or abandonment as opposed to hate (Fenichel, 1944, pp. 145–146; Horney, 1937, pp. 270–274). If love is a "group of two" as Freud (1921, p. 115) surmises, then the altruist feels like an outsider.

There is a problem in this formulation in that while hate and its connection to the object, or sexual relationship drive, was examined by Freud, the relationship of altruism to the sexual relationship wasn't. "The opposite to egoism, altruism, does not, as a concept, coincide with libidinal object-cathexis," Freud writes, "but is distinguished from it by the absence of longings for sexual satisfaction" (Freud, 1917b, p. 418). The question is what accounts for this "absence of longings" and is the complement to the hate that can be mixed with sexuality in egoism. Deutsch (1930) sees the same problem and she holds that it is the primary cause of frigidity and not mere aggression against men as many other analysts hold:

> there is a group of women who constitute the main body figuring in the statistics which give the large percentage of frigidity. The women in question are psychically healthy, and their relation to the world and to their libidinal object is positive and friendly. If questioned about the nature of their experience in coitus, they give answers which show that the conception of orgasm as something to be experienced by themselves is really and truly foreign to them. During intercourse what they feel is a happy and tender sense that they are giving keen pleasure and, if they do not come of a social environment where they have acquired full sexual enlightenment, they are convinced that coitus as a sexual act is of importance only for the man. In it, as in other relations, the woman finds happiness in tender, maternal giving. (Deutsch, 1930, p. 59)

The description of altruism is unmistakable in the group of women Deutsch discusses, but to call their sexual experience masochistic would normally imply that they are being beaten or hurt during sex, and not the absence of sexual satisfaction. I don't have an answer for what accounts for the absence- other than generally noting repression of some kind- but I'm sharing this because it leads to other questions. For example, Freud (1905b) in an early work also pointed to something extra in masochism than the aggressive element, "it is, moreover, a suggestive fact that the existence of the pair of opposites formed by sadism and masochism cannot be attributed merely to the element of aggressiveness" (Freud, 1905b, p. 160). Even when he later hypothesises a primary masochism that becomes deflected to form sadism he still doesn't answer the question of what this primary masochism is when under the sway of eros. To seemingly clear up the confusion, Melanie Klein opposes the death instinct (destructiveness) not to sexuality but to the *life* instinct. She was also on guard against reductionists who wanted to make altruistic impulses mere reaction formations to aggressive ones and held that "the tendency to make reparation ultimately derives from the life instinct" (Klein, 1975, p. 74). Klein's use of "life drive" points to a good solution to the problem but similar logic needs to be applied to the death drive and both need to be established on a more mundane scale.

Freud's work provides an implicit basis for this difference between activity and passivity in the instinct of mastery and the instinct of mimicry. The link of the instinct of mimicry to the passive ideals comes from Freud's linkage of hysteria to the production of art in *Totem and Taboo* (Freud, 1913, p. 73). He contrasts the representation of feelings in art with the philosopher's metaphysical system that is comparable to the delusional system of the paranoiac and the working through of guilt in the compulsive character with religious "ceremonials". Hysteria is found predominantly in women and so this should grant an insight into the passive-feminine position. In a letter to Ferenczi Freud links production of art to an instinct of mimicry:

> the peculiar mimicry of the artist in being able to make his ideas about things similar to them and then being able to re-create these ideas—back to the outside world—anew, in the form of words, materials, colors … In the final analysis, the same roundabout way that is characteristic for the wish fulfillment of the artist in general. (Falzeder & Brabant, 1996, pp. 101–102)

Mimicry here represents a desire for connection that exceeds sexuality as well as exceeding imitation of human bodies to express emotion and a larger "sensibility" in colour, shape, music, and words. Freud also goes into detail about the instinct of mimicry's role in humour, caricature, parody, and travesty in *Jokes and Their Relation to the Unconscious* (Freud, 1905a, p. 200). Sexuality clearly unifies individuals but even if the instinct for mimicry is conceived of as arising from the repression of sexuality, then sexuality must already have in it a tendency for union that is more than a need for bodily contact. In this way eros as more fundamental than sexuality seems appropriate. We'd only have to imagine that this very basic tendency for connection can develop into loyalty, reverence, and the qualities of love that show both lasting connection and idealisation beyond the contagion of feeling in mimicry.

Freud relates mastery to the active position (Freud, 1905b, p. 198; 1924b, p. 163) and Ives Hendrick takes it up as the "work principle" and "primary pleasure in effective integrated performance" in several important articles (Hendrick, 1943a, 1943b, 1951). Although the relation to the caregiver is necessary for the ego to be derived from the id, the child also interacts with the environment around the caregiver in a way that isn't just about self-preservation. There must be some satisfaction in this and if it is part of the masculine or active development then it makes sense to follow Hendrick and talk of pleasure here which isn't from a sexual source. In parallel to the instinct of mimicry, if we make mastery derivative of aggression or destructiveness then there must already be something in aggression that can give satisfaction that is more than the removal of the frustrating object. Satisfaction in power or the will to power seems like the best candidate and Freud (1930) does make the link himself when he writes that

> in the blindest fury of destructiveness, we cannot fail to recognize that the satisfaction of the [destructive] instinct is accompanied by an extraordinarily high degree of narcissistic enjoyment, owing to its presenting the ego with a fulfilment of the latter's old wishes for omnipotence. (Freud, 1930, p. 121)

The narcissistic enjoyment in destroying a rival or displacing these feelings on "trashing one's room", for example, receives best translation in the satisfaction of power. Instead of merely accompanying the destructive drive the will to power, in parallel to eros, appears as the most fundamental and can express itself in destruction and then in mastery. Thus, what we later see as the desire to conquer, find glory, and receive admiration must be imagined as the former desire to conquer chaos to bring about order in the mental processes and body in the instinct for mastery.

II

I believe it is important to point out that many people make the error of considering "ego functions" to be related to matters of IQ in spatial intelligence, logic and arithmetic, and general systematising. However, the ego is also related to "inner perception" and the quality of feeling our emotions, our "impressions of others", pleasure, pain, (etc.). Along with IQ there is EQ (emotional intelligence) and the ability, through mimicry, to intuit the feelings of others by our bodies' resonance with their bodies ("the look" in their eyes and face or tone of their voice). Complex judgements based upon the examination of the interrelations of people can be associated with certain physical expressions and traits so that a wise person can "read" another person very quickly. Early female analysts such as Helene Deutsch (1973) define the passive of the active-passive binary as "an activity directed inward" and sees those of a predominately passive-feminine type as "absolutely independent in such thinking and feeling as relates to their inner life[;] … their capacity for identification [mimicry] is not an expression of inner poverty but of inner wealth" (Deutsch, 1973, p. 196). In contrast, she writes of the "masculinized" or active woman who no longer "draws her wisdom from the deep sources of intuition", who has a "strictly objective approach", and whose "warm, intuitive knowledge has yielded to cold unproductive thinking" (ibid., p. 298). The person with a passive side that was undeveloped or defended against, in Deutsch's assessment, would lack both creative and spontaneous innovations and, for example, wouldn't be a good manager and know what types of people (i.e., characters) can and can't work together.

On one hand it sometimes seems to me that I'm stating something very obvious in saying that people tend to be egoistic and others tend to be altruistic, that some have more IQ or EQ, or are a mixture of the two. However, it's also clear that even someone with emotional intuition has blind spots. People tend to believe the rest of the world to be like them. An egoist will say that women are only attracted to "buff" men, men with money, or some form of power, while an altruist will imagine she can change her "bad boy" boyfriend and bring out the good in him.

Leaving sexual relationships aside, at heart, I believe these two basic positions can be seen in the liberal and conservative political stances. They are based upon whether a person believes others are fundamentally good, deserve social assistance, and marginalised groups should be included or, that others are fundamentally bad, and that other people and outsider groups should help themselves, and shouldn't impinge on the individual's (economic) freedom. In conversations with many liberals they seem to think that "deep down" others really care and, many conservatives believe that love and altruism can only exist in the family or, if they exist outside of it, are too weak in individuals to trust their influence on their motivations. This isn't to say that everyone who is liberal has a passive-altruistic structure because there are later identifications with the parents (in politics, religion, etc.) and various forms of reaction against authority and even rationally self-interested reasons one can have to vote liberal. Similarly, not every liberal politician is primarily a passive-altruist. Rather, my point here is to notice that certain motivations in individuals can be seen in the behaviours of groups and, because of their size and social function, it might be easier for some readers to see these trends in them than in individuals.

One would hope that those who study the science of the mind would appreciate these two poles. Freud (1914a) criticised Adler for "cheerlessly" only seeing egoism or power in every neurosis and having "no place at all for love" (pp. 446–447). However, it often seems like those who explicitly recognise a compliment to egoism and give it central consideration have to leave the psychoanalytic community or are marginalised in it. For example, Sydney Blatt (1998) gives a very impressive review of the literature on these ideas that lists Karen Horney, Heinz Kohut, and Otto Rank, all who wrote about self and other directedness or power being in the self or other (Blatt, 1998, p. 725).[1] Although these people certainly introduced other ideas that might have caused them problems with the psychoanalytic orthodoxy, I think it's important to note that Blatt himself is numbered among a small group of analysts who seem to emphasise the fundamental nature of self-definition *vs.* relatedness, or self as agent *vs.* self in relation, which place egoism and altruism in a broader framework. Additionally, as noted above, Melanie Klein (1975) goes very far in spelling out the passive-feminine position in the attributes of reparation, creativity, and the "helpful attitude" derived from the life instincts (Klein, 1975, p. 201, 207). Even though her two positions of greed and envy *vs.* gratitude and reparation as well as persecutory anxiety and depressive anxiety could very clearly align with the competitive-egoism and affectionate-altruism Klein did little to link her work to Freud's psychic bisexuality and the characterlogical implications have been largely ignored.[2]

Traditionally, the poles of "egoism and altruism" place men as logical and competitive and women as empathic and loving. Again, we can assume that this folk wisdom is noting an emphasis or tendency and this is by no means universal. The issue is that in contrasting the egoistic-competitive and altruistic-affectionate trends of people that "neither of these descriptions goes much below the surface" (Freud, 1930, p. 140). If we don't give in to the temptation to make everything about the will to power and "being on top", and we get over the tendency to want to see everyone as totally unique and special, and allow ourselves to judge characterological similarities and common resistances in people, we still aren't saying much.

I think that Freud was hesitant about tying activity with masculinity and passivity with femininity because he was struggling with a more complex formulation of activity and passivity. Freud's hesitation about employing the terms masculine and feminine stem from two major sources. In the first, Freud makes the salient point that it is sometimes females who are the more active in other species and so the link of penis and activity isn't necessarily a law of nature (Freud, 1933, p. 114). However, he also makes the point that it is the musculature which is linked to the instinct for mastery and the destructive drive and in humans the male, on average, has more developed musculature than women (Freud, 1905b, pp. 198–199; 1923b, p. 41). So, while biological sex and the active position aren't linked in all species, there is a link in the human species that allows us to equate masculine and activity and is no doubt responsible for the popular, folk, and religious wisdom on the subject (i.e., yin and yang in Taoism). To be clear, this doesn't mean that a muscular man necessarily has more active than passive traits. Although everyone dynamically goes through stages of development bisexually what is important for the economics of libido are the fixations one has. We have all met tall and muscular men who are "teddy bears" and thin, aggressive, and mean women.

The second problem Freud raises is the worry to not underestimate the role played by culture. However, as I put forward in the introduction, Freud sees drive-based character as constitutive of an individual's path to happiness and not the influence of culture. So, even when he raises this issue he is led to the conclusion that there is a place of individual character that is observably different than culture's influence:

> there is one particularly constant relation between femininity and instinctual life which we do not want to overlook. The suppression of women's aggressiveness which is prescribed for them constitutionally and imposed on them socially favours the development of powerful masochistic impulses, which succeed, as we know, in binding erotically the destructive trends which have been diverted inwards. Thus masochism, as people say, is truly feminine. But if, as happens so often, you meet with masochism in men, what is left to you but to say that these men exhibit very plain feminine traits? (Freud, 1933, pp. 115–116)

While Freud recognises that culture and "gender roles" do impose themselves upon individuals it shouldn't be forgotten that he researched the desire to be beaten and the desire for castration in male patients (Freud, 1924b, pp. 161–162). In other words, a biological male who possesses a penis can have a phantasy that it's missing and this phantasy can be linked to feelings of "bad conscience" and depression. Thus, although not a universal law of nature, phantasy surrounding intrapsychic relations involving the superego and defensive mechanisms is symbolised by anatomy before sexual difference *qua* "gender role" is established. The concession of psychoanalytic theorists to discourse and narrative-based theories often ignore these findings. Psychic bisexuality may be acknowledged but theorists will claim that gender as a social construction is decisive. However, this ignores that identification with one's anatomical sex and enusing gender role can come into conflict with one's drive based structure. Reich (1990), for example, describes a patient in whom he observes that

> side by side with his de facto feminine-passive nature (mother identification in the ego), he has identified with his father in his ego ideal (father identification in superego and ego ideal). However, he is not able to realize this identification because he lacks a phallic position. He will always be feminine and want to be masculine. A severe inferiority complex, the result of this tension between feminine ego and masculine ego-ideal will ... always [be] present ... (Reich, 1990, p. 164)

The Oedipus complex does introduce sexual difference so that one is open to the normativity of gender, and can mistreated or shamed for not falling in line. However, Freud and classical analysts like Reich don't ignore this fact but see that it must be anchored in one's drive-based psychical constitution. Reich, along with Melanie Klein (1928, p. 174), indicates that development along the active and passive poles can be stunted so that even with sexual difference the active-phallic drives to compete and exercise one's willpower towards admiration and success may not be found in a male. I've come across many male altruists who haven't established egoistic phallic drives and lack the willpower to see through any promises they make. Many have been supported by women for most of their lives and have seemingly never defined themselves by competing with others or seeking to be admired for their skills or independence. If we recognise the lifelong character of the impulsive male altruist then gender roles that are based upon anatomical distinctions can't be as important as some theorists claim.

III

Since Freud's concerns about psychic bisexuality don't diminish the importance of its value, I think his central problem with the concept is that he had insights into feminine forms of egoism and masculine forms of altruism that he was struggling to formalise. The problem with the straightforward formulation of the masculine-egoistic-competitive and feminine-altruistic-restorative poles, is Freud's claim that true women love "only themselves" (Freud, 1914b, pp. 88–90). He claims that "true women" want to have men desire or love them but don't really love them, and if a woman does love it is based upon her having the wish to be like him through what Freud calls "narcissistic object choice". To some extent we have to recognise this as a blind spot in Freud. It shouldn't be forgotten that along with this he said that women are the sex more prone to polymorphic perversions (Freud, 1905b, p. 191) and have a moral deficiency when compared with men. However, Freud, as he should, contradicts himself. He compares being in love with hypnotism and mentions the masochistic trend involved (Freud, 1905b, p. 150) and he clearly identifies masochism as a feminine trait (Freud, 1924b, p. 162). Moreover, Freud (1923b, p. 53) uses melancholia, which is characterised by an excessively cruel superego, as an example of "a pure culture" of the death instinct and this illness is predominately found in women. Furthermore, the apex of morality in doctrines "to turn the other cheek" and "love one's enemies" is associated with moral masochism and again, Freud (1933, p. 116) clearly identifies masochism as feminine. Lastly, quality analysts such as Edith Jacobson have explicitly corrected Freud on his claim that men are the ones who truly love. "In fact, extreme idealization of women, which Freud considers a characteristically masculine attitude" Jacobson writes, "can in my experience be observed more frequently in men who have strong, unconscious female identifications" (Jacobson, 1954b, p. 120).

While acknowledging Freud's prejudice against women, his remark on narcissistic object choice in women also deserves attention as something beyond just a blind spot. It seems clear to me that as much as a person can be narcissistic about her physical and/or intellectual potency she can also be narcissistic about her "looks", attractiveness, or her ability to make or judge beautiful things. We could say that the former, the subject, conquers and that the latter wants to be the object of the subject and "be conquered". The object egoistic tries to make herself the object of the subject (the cause of his desire) whose potency reflects the potency of her beauty. She may put obstacles in the way of her suitor, feigns indifference, and generally "make him work" for her attention or affections. This conserves some of the insight of Freud's remarks on the narcissism of women but allows for a completely different stance to emerge from the altruistic pole. This difference was already put forward as early as 1924. J. Harnik, shows that the relation to phallus exists here too. "To sum up the psychogenetic situation in female narcissism" he writes, "the formula [is]: 'The whole body is equivalent to a genital'". (Hárnik, 1924, p. 79). Harnik also documents that this position is occupied by some men as well: "it is entirely in accordance with our views on bisexuality to assume that a given psychic mechanism operates in both sexes, only more powerfully in the one than in the other ..." (ibid., p. 71). Harnik cites male body builders and the figure of Hercules as examples of men who want their "beauty" to cause desire.

The complement to defensive narcissism in the altruistic pole of the personality is tied to masochism. Conceptually, I think it is better to use the complementary figure of Echo in the myth of Narcissus and contrast defensive narcissism and echoism, and save masochism to be paired with sadism as a specific kind of behaviour. Freud brings up defensive masochism (echoism) in several places in regard to hypnotism and love turning into fascination or bondage but, there is also an ego drive aspect of this in which we say someone is self-effacing, a people pleaser, a pushover, (etc.). I understand this to be what goes under the heading of "feminine masochism" in much of the classic literature. Nietzsche's observation that someone can seek to devote themselves to another's perfection instead of being an agent on their own can also be extended to the ego sphere. We can note people who give up their personality (individual thoughts or tastes) in order to be a spokesperson for a certain group, people who always fuss about everyone else being well fed and comfortable without concern for themselves, and people whose 'bleeding hearts' often ensure the mental health field is well-staffed despite its low pay.

In addition to "feminine masochism", we can point to someone who echoistically (masochistically) needs the approval of others and suffers when he's not liked, or others haven't appreciated his uniqueness or style. Freud points to the object position of the altruist when he writes:

> loving—being loved, corresponds exactly to the transformation from activity to passivity. … according as the object or the subject is replaced by an extraneous one, what results is the active aim of loving or the passive one of being loved—the latter remaining near to narcissism. (Freud, 1915, p. 133)

Freud writes that being loved is "near to narcissism" but, again, one must pay attention to the phenomenology. Just because a person talks a lot and seems to draw a lot of attention it doesn't mean that they are establishing their power or dominance. Here qualities like charm, endearment, exuberance, or style are in order. Self-consciousness in the non-philosophical sense of attempting to make oneself interesting through a subculture or imitating someone is an illustration of the echoism, or pains one will go through, to be regarded as interesting for others. Although the will to power is arguably involved in this, the sense of belonging has much more emphasis in the motivation.

Early analysts like Wilhelm Reich saw this motivation at work in their patients. Reich writes of one who had the "desire to be a child who is loved by everyone—at the same time realizing that he himself neither wanted to love nor was able to love" (Reich, 1990, p. 113). Theodore Reik also claims that anyone who has read Goethe's biography "will gain the impression that for him the feeling of being loved had, from childhood to old age, been more important than the need to love"

(Reik, 1963, p. 3). Thus, we have a subject altruist who risks emotional investment in love and an object altruistic who desires to "be loved" by the subject—to be the cause of delight in him or her. Freud aligns the subject position with the feminine when he notes the masochism in love (hypnotism) and self-sacrifice for the benefit of others so they can feel a sense of belonging.

If the object egoistic is feminine, as Harnik suggests, then, deductively, we can place the object altruistic as the masculine object form. Loewenstein (1935) links impotence with phallic passivity, in which one desires the object to be the sexual aggressor, as opposed to being a feminine identification. Additionally, the picaresque hero, who doesn't trade on his superior skill, intelligence, or potency, but on his wit or charm, is most often depicted as a male. I understand that, historically, to say that the hero is most often male doesn't meant that much, because of the oppression of women that would limit their expression in this kind of way. However, the example is more important in order to orient my reader's perception to the sensibility I have in mind. As with everything in this book, I'm trying to express the most coherent theory of the psychoanalytic thought that has resonated with me. To leave hypothesis and intuition for fact will require that the phenomenology described is routinely paired with the depth structures, erotogenic zones, and symbols found in the patient's phantasy, the artist's creation, and the mystic's mythology. Neuroscience will do doubt have something to say in this as well.

If the two subject positions can be captured by the two political stances, the two object positions can be captured by the two major appeals of entertainment coverage in the media. The object egoistic is concerned with beauty and being the cause of desire to the subject and the entertainment industry has always been filled with people more known for their beauty than for their talent. Celebrity magazines sometimes seem geared to showing them without make-up or looking badly in order to make the reader think she may be more beautiful. Sometimes there is a write up that shows the "beauty queen" as "down to earth" by having certain tastes or values that relegate physical beauty to a secondary role. The object altruistic is concerned with individuality and whether it's through humour, charisma, or the ability to inspire others there are many entertainers who similarly lack talent diversity in their art (i.e., play the same role in acting) or have too much diversity (i.e., change with fashion and don't mine their own passions in music). They succeed because they cause delight in others, not because they have the talent to really represent different types of people or their own feelings.

In order to flesh out these four positions, I'd like to examine how they would appear at the phallic level of development as showcased in the second generation of Greek Gods. I want to also add the further division between Freud's "narcissistic man" with an economic cathexis of his "internal mental functions" and Freud's "man of action" who tries his strength in the external world (Freud, 1930, pp. 83–84). The former can be identified with the abstractions of math, research in science, or is preoccupied with culture (art, religion, philosophy) more than people. For the latter, the "internal mental functions" are of secondary importance and points of view or taste are adopted through identification with others more than through argument or subjective resonance. The narcissistic man, in this usage, is identified with the *mind* and less at home in the body and the man of action is identified with the *body* and less at home with the mind.

In subject egoism, the body form is Ares, the physically strong and competitive God of war, who is most often portrayed as a man in the prime of his life. He seeks glory in conquest and his excellence is clearly in physical battle. Today, along with athletes, for example, the modern equivalent might be a businessman who frequents the gym. Business shares many terms with warfare and class climbing provides an opportunity for increased admiration from others. The mind form is Hephaestus, the God of metalworking and stone masonry, whose body is crippled and thus exemplifies intellectual dominance as opposed to the physical dominance of Ares. His excellence is in his inventions and intelligence, although in today's world this man might be an innovator in technology or science rather than a blacksmith.

In the object egoistic position, the body form is Aphrodite, the goddess of beauty and sexual desire. She is described as physically beautiful, sensuous, and seductive. On the mind side is Athena, the goddess of handicrafts and wisdom. Her interest is in secondary finery (beautiful adornments) as opposed to the physical embodiment of sexuality represented by Aphrodite. This is analogous to Hephaestus who made the implements for those who fought. Additionally, with the focus on the mind, Athena would stand back and observe desire between people, as compared to Aphrodite who lives it out. It's possible that EQ shouldn't be fully aligned with the altruistic pole and that a theory of mind appears here in regards to unmasking potential rivals or how to sustain the other's desire. Understanding the psychology of the enemy with whom your state is at war seems a likely candidate for as to what gives Athena another facet as the goddess of war.

In subject altruism, Artemis, the goddess of childbirth and the hunt, represents the body form. I have interpreted her interest in hunting, which would be a masculine occupation with the Greeks, as an expression of her devotion to carrying on the work or perfection of a love object. Her status as a virgin would indicate that she loved her father and has remain devoted to him ever since. Freud (1923b) writes:

> analysis very often shows that a little girl, after she has had to relinquish her father as a love-object, will bring her masculinity into prominence and identify herself with her father (that is, with the object which has been lost), instead of with her mother. (Freud, 1923b, p. 32)

An example of this can be seen with Freud's own daughter Anna, who, ensured that her father's theories and approach lived on, although it also meant attacking those who may have been true to Freud's ideas in spirit. Hermes, the messenger God of cunning wiles, is the mind form of subject altruism. His devotion to the family of Gods instead of his own personal glory illustrates his service to an idea, the group, as opposed to a particular individual. The political activist who brings the messages and stories of marginalised groups to centres of power might be a contemporary example.

In the object altruistic category, the body form is Dionysus, the God of wine, parties, and festivals. Although it may be emphasised more in the Roman version of Bacchus, I think most people know outgoing social types who seek to cause delight and restore the group to good spirits. He may be the centre of attention but it's not on account of how potent or handsome he is (i.e., defensively narcissistic). What I want to capture is that Dionysus, in one facet, could be seen as a "people person", even though other facets of his personality are dark or self-destructive. Apollo, the God of music, healing, prophecies, and poetry, typifies the mind dimension of the object altruist. He illustrates a more esoteric ability to gain the approval of others by touching something deeper in them than the Dionysian approach. This person wants to guess your astrological sign or write you a sonnet to be interesting and cause you delight. As opposed to Dionysian type who forms his tastes through identifications with others, the Appollonian type may identify with more esoteric ideas or tastes separated in time or space from one's group. In this way, the Appollonian type may touch upon the sphere of judgement of beauty that was aligned with object egoism. Additionally, in contrast to Athena's wisdom, in judging the desires of others, the Apollonian often refers to the "energies" or sensibilites that others have.

These qualitative distinctions are of central importance because, as I'll explore in the third chapter, the Oedipus complex represents a developmental point at which the egoistic and altruistic poles have intermingled to the point of being nearly balanced. However, a passive-aggressive type, who doesn't get angry or demand others to do what he wants but, instead, tries to prey upon their guilt or pity, demonstrates egoism and aggression but its form is much different then the open aggression and demands found in the egoistic pole. Conversely, in an active-affectionate type, altruism and affection appear only for one's children or those who are under one's power, who are seen as extensions of oneself. This altruism and affection wouldn't be mistaken for the compassion and enjoyment of tenderness, cuteness, sentimentality found in the altruistic pole. Moreover, despite the emphasis an individual may have on one of the poles, or libidinal positions, psychopathology may appear from a less dominant position because of the specific ego or object drive that receives an injury or frustration that leads to defusion.

Earlier in the chapter I linked art to the feminine and the instinct of mimicry in the altruist. This came about because egoism, competition, and mastery are linked in Freud's work and I was searching for a parallel in altruism. Above, I also noted Athena's investment in beauty and I wouldn't wish to suggest that art only springs from the altruistic pole of the personality. Rather, I'd like to suggest that designation of the sublime and the beautiful in art are made more intelligible in appreciating the different attitudes of the egoist and altruist. Nietzsche also captures this difference in his Appollonian *vs.* Dionysian approach to art. He writes:

> what is the meaning of the conceptual opposites which I have introduced into aesthetics, Apollonian and Dionysian, both conceived as kinds of frenzy? The Apollonian frenzy excites the eye above all,

so that it gains the power of vision. The painter, the sculptor, the epic poet are visionaries par excellence. In the Dionysian state, on the other hand, the whole affective system is excited and enhanced: so that it discharges all its means of expression at once and drives forth simultaneously the power of representation, imitation, trans-figuration, transformation, and every kind of mimicking and act-ing. The essential feature here remains the ease of metamorphosis, the inability *not* to react (similar to certain hysterical types who also, upon any suggestion, enter into *any* role) ... It is impossible for the Dionysian type not to understand any suggestion; he does not overlook any sign of an affect; he possesses the instinct of under-standing and guessing in the highest degree, just as he commands the art of communication in the highest degree. He enters into any skin, into any affect: he constantly transforms himself. (Nietzsche, 1982b, pp. 519–520)

I want to emphasise, again, that the Gods have much richer personalities than the single facet I'm using to illustrate the phallic drives. Everyone is bisexual even if one of the poles of the person-ality hasn't fully developed and a person may have fixations in both poles in their personality. Therefore, in earlier stages Apollo may very well represent egoistic functions. Going beyond the genre identifi-cations Nietzsche gives us (i.e., Dionysian painting, sculpture, and poetry) and the symbols of the eye and skin (although psychoana-lytically valuable), the two approaches are captured more simply as the contrast between mastery and mimicry. The impulses to control/possess the object, engage with it systematically, with symmetry, or based upon some imposed order are important in the Apollonian. Making representations that are identified with what is the most desirable, clean, or beautiful defines Apollonian art. The impulses to resonate/merge with the object, engage with it based upon its emo-tional make-up, and to sketch this emotional make-up in many differ-ent ways or display many different objects are the foundation of the Dionysian. Furthermore, to relate the human body to the form of a tree, house, or anything, or making representations that are identified with what is delightful in its uniqueness or novelty is an expression of the Dionysian. Although this interpretation deserves its own scholarly study, my hope here is not to convince so much as to direct my reader to the existence of such distinctions that oppose the current fashion of semiotic interpretation of the arts.

IV

Now that I've given some cultural examples of the four libidinal positions, I'd like to return to the subject that initially drove me to this research and give an example of the importance of psychic bisexuality for the clinic. My research into psychic bisexuality began with my efforts to make sense of hysteria. On one hand, some analysts seem so confident in using such labels in discussing their patients but, on the other, the scholarship has long shown a problem:

> it is well known that psychoanalytic theory faces difficulty when it attempts to relate either character modes or symptom complexes to any one diagnostic entity. The terms, hysteria, hysterical character, etc., are so loosely defined and applied so promiscuously that their application to diagnostic categories has become meaningless. The use of these labels for evaluation, analyzability, or prognosis has become tantamount to predicting a throw of the dice. (Easser & Lesser, 1965, pp. 392–393)

Without being able to simply attach hysteria to conversion symptoms, the term must apply to behaviours or character. However, the problem is that many types of behaviour are called hysterical. In this state of affairs one can either pretend these problems don't exist and go on applying the term as he has been taught, or, as is often the case, one can give up on characterology and claim that the individual is wholly unique. Between dogmatic assertions of *the* hysterical behaviour and the post-modern uniqueness of the individual, there is a middle ground that follows common language in matching different behaviours with different motivations. What I have in mind for this is the impression when sitting with a patient that she has a sense of self-respect or pride derived from the feeling that her physical beauty and/or aesthetic or spiritual refinements are special or superior to those of others. Jacobson cites the "uncommon narcissistic pride in their 'inner values,' their moral integrity, the high level of their standards, [and] the relentless strength of their ideal values which turn out to represent, unconsciously, their 'inner penis' in such women" (Jacobson, 1954b, pp. 118–119). Karl

Abraham doesn't describe the phenomenology of his patients but recounts common object egoistic phantasies in his patients:

> in some of our patients we come across phantasies which refer to the possibility of a recognition of the man and to the formulation of conditions under which the patient, after their fulfilment, would be prepared to reconcile herself to her femininity. I mention first of all a condition I have met with many times; it runs: "I could be content with my femininity if I were absolutely the most beautiful of all women." All men would lie at the feet of the most beautiful woman, and the female narcissism would consider this power not a bad compensation for the defect so painfully perceived ... (Abraham, 1922, pp. 25–26)

Although Abraham relegates these phantasies to responses to the castration conflict instead of seeing them as motivations that still exist in non-pathological states, this is his "depth interpretation". There are object egoists who we can judge to be motivated by the desire to be viewed as sexually attractive, or as someone you wish you could win the love of, without revenge or triangulation coming into play. Abraham goes on to talk of a second major phantasy that women suffering from the castration complex possess, which is the wish "to be unique" (ibid., pp. 25–26). This motivation finds purchase in the object altruistic (OA) position. In an article entitled "A reevaluation of hysterical relatedness" (1986) Marylou Lionells paints a picture of the histrionic-hysteric that provides a foil to the object egoistic (OE) hysteric. She uses the terms "self-as-agent" and "self-in-relation" for what I've identified as egoistic vs. altruistic trends in the personality and places the hysteric in the latter category (Lionells, 1986, p. 577). She quotes Freud's position that "being loved, is the most important thing in life" for this character type (ibid., p. 571). She also does a literature review in which she supports a view of "emotionality as an interpersonal tool designed to elicit approval" and her findings are as follows:

> the hysteric seeks sustained interest, excitement, and especially approval ... while all interacting persons manipulate others to fulfil personal needs, the hysteric achieves his particular goal by seeming relatively helpless and dependent ... To the extent that I'm hysterical I care more that you like me than that you agree with

> me or even understand me … hysterical approval seeking is a
> search for emotional holding, though phrased as if help is what is
> needed. The hysteric can behave quite independently as long as a
> fantasy is maintained that another presides over that activity as a
> parent, authority, seat of power, and fount of love. (Lionells, 1986,
> pp. 571–573)

Instead of the distance we find with the OE, whose pride can remove
her from relationships, the OA hysteric attempts to get emotional holding, by making herself unique which can manifest as portraying herself
as what she thinks is interesting or edgy, being vulnerable, or by being
sexual. The OE hysteric wants to be beautiful or have superior taste
and is resentful towards men for her power not causing desire in them.
The OA hysteric's emphasis is very different. "Being cute (not necessarily beautiful), alert, responsive, and cheerful are common attributes",
Lionell writes, "budding hysterics often seem to have an innate sense of
humour. They spontaneously clown and entertain. They show a quick
wit, making use of analogy and metaphor …" (ibid., p. 583). However,
what can be endearing or charming in health can become dramatic
and sloppy in pathology. Similarly the desire to establish one's uniqueness, inspire others, and generally be cause of the other's delight can
cause the OA hysteric to move on from one person to the next to seek
approval. In Sachs "One of the motive factors in the formation of the
super-ego in women" (1929) we are given a classic portrait of the OA
hysteric. However, Sachs emphasises the dilettantism of the OA, whose
potential lack of egoistic drives mean that skill and knowledge aren't
mastered, without an eye for the strengths in EQ or spontaneity that the
OA may posses.

The object egoistic and altruistic relations to the castration complex
are also documented by Wilhelm Reich in the way that they show up in
the transference. He differentiates between a compulsive and hysteric
character:

> the woman suffering from hysteria, for example, will be appre-
> hensively silent and behave timidly; the woman having a com-
> pulsive neurosis will be obstinately silent or behave in a cold,
> haughty way towards the analyst. The transference resistance
> employs various means in warding off the positive transference …
> the woman suffering from hysteria will always defend herself

in a way expressive of anxiety, while the woman suffering from a compulsive neurosis will always defend herself aggressively, no matter what unconscious content is on the verge of breaking through.... That they hysterical character is easily excited can be inferred from the appearance as a whole. The appearance of the compulsive character, on the other hand, suggests restraint. (Reich, 1990, p. 51, 205)

Although Reich doesn't talk about the specific motivations involved, his account does follow the active-egoistic and passive-altruistic binary. Reich's compulsive is what classical Freudians and Lacanians usually identify as hysterics. Freud's Dora, for example, would much be much better described as cold, haughty, aggressive, etc. than as timid, erratic, or easily excited. I've come to understand that analysts who don't recognise both types are usually reductive and use a single libidinal pole to explain motivation. When Lacan describes the hysteric as not wanting the man to get off on her and getting off on leaving him sexually unsatisfied, my experience is that this is coupled with OE pride and competition between subject and object egoist (Fink, 1997, p. 127).[3] The OA or histrionic-hysteric may have competitive feelings with other women regarding her beauty but there is more emphasis on her being cute or endearing, her wanting to be interesting or unique and causing delight, rather than causing desire. When there is a lack of sex in a relationship with her it is because she no longer idealises the object and is going on to get emotional holding elsewhere as opposed to an idealisation of self and aggression towards the object (and protest of sexual difference). However, these two different characterological views still don't encompass all of what has been called hysterical and they are much more of a beginning than the final word on the subject.

Lastly, as Freud, Reich, or any person of decent judgement will point out, the bodily comportment—the severity or seriousness of the compulsive *vs.* the exuberance or excitability of the histrionic—is as important here as the motivational structure. "If we yield to the legitimate need to distinguish particular types in this multiplicity", Freud (1931b) writes,

we shall at the start have the choice as to what characteristics and what points of view we shall take as the basis of our

> differentiation. For that purpose physical qualities will doubtless
> serve no less well than mental ones; the most valuable distinctions
> will be those which promise to present a regular combination of
> physical and mental characteristic. (Freud, 1931b, p. 217)

Reich has been the only student of Freud's to begin the exploration of
the correlation of physiognomy to the different motivational structures.
With the anti-authoritarian move in culture and the "sexual revolution"
since Freud, it seems that his insights into the repression of sexuality in
the Victorian era covered up a more primitive repression of the body in
general that still has to be reckoned with in psychoanalytic thought. Id
forms of aggression or affection have both a mental and physical form
and, therefore, must involve some physical suppression. In my opinion,
anyone with an intellectual conscience will be aware that the narcissistic and echoistic injuries and disappointments in love, that lead to a
diminishment in our relations with others, will be followed by chronic
musculature tensions and changes in the body. Clenched jaws, stiff legs,
tight belly, raised shoulders, etc. can appear later in life and are a valuable avenue to approach psychopathology for many patients.

I haven't attempted to be exhaustive in this description of two
varieties of hysteria. For example, in the next chapter I discuss the
etiology of the "genital" stage hysteric in contrast to the phallic characterology examined here. Instead my intention was to direct my
reader to the important division in hysteria that I soon came to see
in my investigation. By referring back to the work of major analysts
that have acknowledged the difference between object egoism and
altruism in their work without formalising it, I hope to have pointed
to a phenomenology beyond a singular idiosyncratic judgement. In
formalising the phenomenology of libidinal types, my hope is to provide a framework that will allow other character types to be investigated along a horizontal axis and not just a simple vertical axis of
psychosexual development (oral, anal, phallic, etc.). Again, between
dogmatic assertions that the hysteric is defined by X behaviour or
that every individual is unique there is a middle ground. This middle
ground follows common language and respects that many different
motivations and desires can be ascribed to people. Just as people have
different IQs, they also have different EQs. The ability to perceive different feelings and motivations in people is the only direction that
psychoanalytic characterology can take if it is to survive, and I hope

this chapter gives those who possess this "inner wealth" the courage to follow it.

Notes

1. One Kohutian writes: "one pole consists of the person's most basic ambitions, goals and self-esteem, which develop out of the young child's grandiosity and exhibitionism being mirrored and affirmed. The other pole consists of the person's core values and guiding principles, which develop out of the young child's idealizing and feeling merged with the 'omnipotence' of the parent. A creative 'tension arc' develops between these two poles, motivating each person to fulfill the unique potentialities established in the basic design of his or her nuclear self. Hence, this model suggests an energic flow between two oppositely charged poles, and underscores a relational matrix of psychic energy which provides the most basic human motivation. Thus, 'the needs of the self', rather than the demands of the instincts, motivate inner activity, growth and movement" (Kill, 1986, p. 20). Horney talks of the passive-feminine, compliant or self-effacing trends that "lie in the direction of goodness, sympathy, love, generosity, unselfishness, humility; while egotism, ambition, callousness, unscrupulousness, wielding of power are abhorred" (Horney, 1950, p. 54). In contrast, the active-masculine or expansive trends impart a sense of moral goodness for merely not hurting, stealing, or killing others (thou shalt not). Also see Sachs, 1929.
2. Interestingly, Klein herself has called for this kind of characterological work to be done: "character analysis has always been an important and very difficult part of analytic therapy. It is, I believe, through tracing back certain aspects of character formation to the early processes I have described that we can, in a number of cases, effect far-reaching changes in character and personality" (Klein, 1975, p. 234).
3. Someone who is manifestly an object egoist may have her altruistic pole operating in latent ways. In my clinical experience with substance abuse I have worked with object egoists who can be in relationships with passive men in which the man "is walking on eggshells" and is afraid of their anger or of losing their love. This follows Freud's (1926a) findings that castration anxiety for (altruistic) women is based upon "loss of love" (p. 143). These patients can candidly admit that the man is like "the girl" in the relationship and that they were previously in relationships with men in which they felt the way their current boyfriend does. This appears to be a form of projective identification in which they identify with the parental imago and force their anxiety

into another. Projective identification in this vein is further discussed in Chapter Three. However, along with the suggestion that an object egoist is seeking to cause love in another that she won't return, Freud's concept of narcissistic object choice also covers an operation similar to projective identification. Freud (1914b) writes that women "still retain the capacity of longing for a masculine ideal—an ideal which is in fact a survival of the boyish nature that they themselves once possessed" (p. 90). I have encountered female patients with strong anxiety who seem not to function on the egoistic pole of their personality. In analytic work the man they stay with, who often cheats on them and threatens them when he's told to leave, is described in terms that they applied to their former way of living. He is "lawless" and "not afraid of anything" as they once were and, in my experience, they must recognise themselves in him before they can quit the relationship.

CHAPTER TWO

"An array of ideal values": ego psychology and the destiny of the Oedipus complex

In this chapter I argue that American ego psychology has led psychoanalysts astray regarding the nature of the superego. Although it has made some valuable contributions to psychoanalytic theory, ego psychologists from Heinz Hartmann to David Milrod, who I examine here as the most recent exponent of these views, claim that the dissolution of the Oedipus complex creates a conflict-free zone in the ego. The former dependence upon the parents becomes internalised as "autonomy" and the individual chooses his own "ideal values" as the basis of the superego. This is a view of a primarily *atomistic* or separate individual whose relation to himself and others is based upon the values he chooses. In contrast, Freud's position, I argue, doesn't claim any such autonomy for the individual after the Oedipus complex. Instead, the dependency upon the parents is continued as dependency upon their internalised images, or imagos, that mediate the individuals relation to father-substitutes in the community based upon their superior strength or potency or their greater reputation or Prestige. The dependence on these substitutes then becomes dependency upon fellow citizens in one's community and then moves on to the tradition of one's culture. No "conflict-free zone" is posited in Freud's model. Humans don't choose to be political animals but are driven to be so.

I understand the contrast between the ego psychological interpretation of Freud and the position I put forward here as a refined version of an earlier debate. In "A difficulty in the path of psychoanalysis" Freud (1917a) claims that psychoanalysis is a blow to the narcissism of humanity. This blow, he argues, is greater than Darwin's discovery that man is an evolved ape, which itself was greater than Copernicus' finding that the earth isn't the centre of the universe. Following the philosophers Schopenhauer and Nietzsche, Freud argues that our:

> mind is not a simple thing; on the contrary, it is a hierarchy of super-ordinated and subordinated agencies, a labyrinth of impulses striving independently of one another towards action, corresponding with the multiplicity of instincts and of relations with the external world, many of which are antagonistic to one another and incompatible. (Freud, 1917a, p. 141)

Although this passage might remind one of the description of the id as a seething cauldron Freud is, in fact, talking about the ego. What Freud has in mind here are such things as the conflict between the ego and object drives and the superego. For example, one may love, or feel devoted to a friend, but also compete with him at the same time; or one may want to be in a position of leadership or authority while also feeling that one hasn't acquired the necessary knowledge or skill to deserve it. Freud doesn't write about a single superordinate agency internalised after the Oedipus complex here but instead "a hierarchy of superordinated and subordinated agencies" that exist throughout development. Additionally, in other places Freud explicitly holds that there are multiple imagos that have formed the superego throughout psychosexual development (Freud, 1923b, p. 48; 1933, p. 64). Thus, this model of the mind in conflict—a mind that is made up of multiple subordinate (ego and object drives) and superordinate (superego) agencies—continues throughout Freud's work.

In his late phase, Freud began to outline the characterological expression of an individual's drive-based or instinctual constitution in greater specificity. How we strive for happiness isn't determined by choice, but by the ego and object drives, superego, and various fixations and adaptations formed throughout the process of psychosexual development. These different factors determine the individual's *economy of libido* or how his psychic energy can be directed. Freud (1930) writes:

happiness, in the reduced sense in which we recognize it as possible, is a problem of the *economics of the individual's libido*. There is no golden rule which applies to everyone: every man must find out for himself in what particular fashion he can be saved. All kinds of different factors will operate to direct his choice. It is a question of how much real satisfaction he can expect to get from the external world, how far he is led to make himself independent of it, and, finally, how much strength he feels he has for altering the world to suit his wishes. In this, *his psychical constitution will play a decisive part, irrespectively of the external circumstances*. The man who is predominantly erotic will give first preference to his emotional relationships to other people; the narcissistic man, who inclines to be self-sufficient, will seek his main satisfactions in his internal mental processes; the man of action will never give up the external world on which he can try out his strength … success is never certain, for that depends on the convergence of many factors, perhaps on none more than on the *capacity of the psychical constitution to adapt its function to the environment* and then to exploit that environment for a yield of pleasure. A person who is born with a specially unfavourable *instinctual constitution*, and who has not properly undergone the transformation and rearrangement of his libidinal components which is indispensable for later achievements, will find it hard to obtain happiness from his external situation, especially if he is faced with tasks of some difficulty. (Freud, 1930, pp. 83–84, emphasis mine)

Freud emphasises the variety of idiosyncratic approaches people take toward the world; each is "driven" and unable to switch drives or their concomitant attitudes. An individual, for example, doesn't choose to be ambitious but is active-egoistically motivated or driven to have a reputation of being successful or powerful. And the ego ideal causes him to suffer inferiority or jealousy of others if his name isn't mentioned with admiration. Additionally, someone can be a "people person" and passive-altruistically want approval from, or to be well liked, for his humorous stories or connection to popular people, and suffer feelings of aloneness or self-pity if this doesn't occur. Freud (1931b) is clear that the ego and object drives that give the erotic, narcissistic, man of action, and other types their path of happiness can exist, and form conflicts, in a single individual (pp. 218–219).

However, as I expressed in the last chapter, the drive or motivational structure will often have an emphasis on a certain libidinal position: a position can be arrested in development; or later defences can be erected against it. Moreover, along with this horizontal dimension there is a vertical axis (phallic, anal, etc.) in which the difference between being disposed, for example, towards action or being a self-sufficient, intellectual type becomes salient for each type. Scientists, artists, or generally introverted people may prefer dealing with art-objects, mathematics, or their daydreams rather than the natural world.[1] This vertical axis is the subject of the next chapter.

In this chapter, the focus is on Freud's *Copernican revolution* on the rational chooser model in which the individual chooses what he *will* do and is responsible for "willing" to do it or not. The ambitious man is driven to demand the recognition or respect of others and, in actuality, is *not* "free" to choose. He experiences jealousy when he hears that his peers are wealthier in money or reputation than he is. He suffers feelings of inferiority or self-contempt (i.e., tension between the ego and ego ideal) if he fails to equalise the situation and earn the esteem or the respect of those in the community that he is driven to possess. Instead of a merely phenomenological account I will return to central concepts like the superego and Oedipus complex and show how Freud conceived of them as intersubjective, or, as making individuals primarily related to others in the community.

David Milrod agrees that drives to individual happiness exist outside of will or rational choice. He does, however, stress that it is possible to rationally choose ethical values. In Milrod's account an individual chooses and measures himself against values that pertain to what kind of person he or she would like to be. This choice is unrelated to a drive-motivated campaign for happiness but is instead a desire "to live up [to] the ego ideal and its abstract, depersonified standards[;] the concern is for how we deal with others, which is the fundamental focus of morality" (Milrod, 2002, p. 137). However, I will show that this view is very much different than Freud's. In the active egoistic individual the guilt conscience is distinct from earlier forms of conscience because one can feel bad about intentions to perform prohibited behaviour, while in earlier development one doesn't judge oneself regarding intentions to perform prohibited actions but rather has "remorse [that] relates only to a deed that has been done" (Freud, 1930, p. 131).

In Freud's account the imago, and not "ideal values", is what first provides the basis for the values of the superego *qua* guilt conscience. Values are created by the Talion rule that the anxiety, pain, or unpleasure caused in another person, who occupies the imago relation, are returned upon one's self by the imago. Freud compares this operation to Kant's categorical imperative (Freud, 1913, p. 22; 1924b, p.167). Fairness is not a value that is chosen so much as an imago relation from which one observes oneself as equal to others in the community. Freud does recognise that ideal values do come to play a part in the later development of latency but he doesn't represent the individual as autonomously choosing them. Instead, the individual who develops to latency forms an identity comprised of different "group minds" of race, class, creed, and nationality that contain certain mores (Freud, 1921, p. 129). "The child's super-ego is in fact constructed on the model not of its parents but of its parents 'super-ego'", Freud (1933) writes, and "the contents which fill it are the same and it becomes the vehicle of tradition and of all the time-resisting judgments of value which have propagated themselves in this manner from generation to generation" (Freud, 1933, p. 67). Thus, the conscience that was dependent on parental imagos later becomes dependant upon traditions, or the individual mores taken from the group minds, and Freud doesn't reference autonomy or the rational choosing of values in these developments.

Since the notion of an autonomous value-choosing development in the individual doesn't have much support in Freud's model, I argue that it is better understood as the re-emergence of the rational chooser model best associated with Descartes' mind/body dualism. The strength of Freud's Copernican revolution on the rational chooser model is that individual characterological differences are explained by psychosexual development and that this provides material for culture to grow from instead of it arising *ex-nihilo*. While this idea will be examined more in the appendix, in this chapter I argue that Milrod's model can't account for the diversity of character types in phases of history that don't offer the many different cultural traditions contemporary globalisation allows us access to. An individual may behave like a stoic, a hedonist, a liberal, etc. without having studied the "ideal values" that come from the texts or formalised principles of these groups. Moreover, an individual living in a late capitalist economy in which globalisation and individual freedoms allow access to different world views and religions can often be seen to be rationalising his character-based motivations and feelings by identifying as an adherent of a view. Ultimately, I argue that Freud's subtler position on superego development, dependency, and conflict allows for more rigorous interdisciplinary discourse and offers more nuanced clinical implications for pathology.

In the course of conducting these arguments, I will only focus on what I termed the subject egoistic libidinal position in which competition with others to gain recognition or admiration for one's skills or intellectual potency is the major source of self-esteem (or "narcissistic libido"). This attitude towards others is generally accepted by most people and most references in the literature concern the active position of the boy, so tracing its developments will create a foundation in the central concepts of classical psychoanalysis that will allow for me to add the other libidinal positions in a later work.

There are many analysts who would criticise a project that returns to the superego, even if it is to criticise and expand on the ego psychology tradition. To some extent, writing about "the superego" and the structural theory seems quaint or misconceived. Some analysts criticise Freud's view of conscience as misogynistic, and others draw attention towards reparative impulses and morality that are different from the guilt conscience Freud established after the oedipal stage (for example, Sagan (1989), *Freud, Women, Morality*). I think that they all have valid points to make. However, I don't think this means that Freud's view of conscience is wrong but, rather, that it is one-sided and based upon the special attention he gave to the boy's development. The guiding principle for the separation of the active-egoistic and passive-altruistic forms of conscience comes from Hans Sachs (1929) contrast between the "thou shalt not" and "thou shalt" differences he aligned with the active and passive poles (p. 46). I've come to understand this difference along these lines. The egoist considers himself a good person for what he doesn't do to a stranger: "I don't kill you, rob you, or treat you worse than I treat your equals (i.e., unfairly)—therefore I am good" ("thou shalt not"). The altruist considers himself a good person for what he does for a stranger: "I am nice to you, make you feel welcome, or I help you to get yourself back on the track of striving for happiness—therefore I am good". Even though I won't explore the difference in this chapter, again, I'm aware that there is an important passive dimension to the superego that I am leaving out and that made previous discussions warrant the criticism they received.

I

In David Milrod's model, children internalise parental authority at the point of the Oedipus complex (Milrod, 2002, p. 140). After this transition, the child can rationally choose his own moral values in regard to the direction-giving aspect of the ego ideal and the prohibitory aspect of the conscience. The pre- and post-oedipal break thus hinges on this new ability to engage in rational choice in regard to morality. The pre-oedipal child, in Milrod's account is only conditioned to fear parental punishment and does not have a conscience. Furthermore, in regard to the ego ideal, the child only imitates authority figures in varying degrees of complexity in order to participate in their power and isn't self-determining as with the chosen values of the ego ideal. This fear of parental punishment and imitative identification with parental power are conceived of as "superego forerunners" and the superego proper, comprised of conscience and ego ideal, only forms as a result of the Oedipus complex. Milrod understands this change of affairs, from forerunner to superego proper, as the move of self-observation that is located in the ego to self-observation being anchored in the superego. I believe the superego forerunner *vs.* superego view invites a strong comparison with the Lacanian view of the ideal ego and ego ideal and will discuss it to further contrast Freud's position.

Milrod (2002) defines the ego ideal as a structure that helps to recover the sense of narcissistic perfection in the infant that is lost on account of the "capacity to exercise critical self-judgment and because of the inevitable accumulation over time of the criticism of others" (Milrod, 2002, p. 132). The infant becomes aware of its dependence on, and the difference of power between, it and its parents and then, through identification with them it attempts to regain some of its lost power.

For Milrod the earliest version of the projection of perfection is when object and self-representations differentiate from each other. A self-representation is a concept originated by Hartmann (1950) to differentiate the ego as perceptual consciousness system from the ego as receiver of cathexis (i.e., narcissistic libido) that is part of a self-esteem system in which various feelings about oneself are expressed (for example "I am bad, dirty, and unacceptable"). There are various self-representations that are created through psychosexual development and they are paired with object representations that hold the child's immature pictures of the parent's power. This terminology appears to be a replacement of Freud's use of the concept of the imago and description of superego tensions of conscience and the failure to live up to the imago's perfection, on one hand, and used to account for defensive operations of the ego that further complicate the superego operations, on the other. Freud's general view of the pre-oedipal superego and its imago determined nature will be presented in the following sections.

In Milrod's account, the child's initial sense of perfection is projected or "transferred" upon the parents when the narcissistic blow of recognising one's own helplessness occurs. This is followed by a longing to be like the parents. This longing is first gratified by a phantasy of merger comprised of imitations of the behaviour of the object of perfection. Milrod gives the example of a little girl putting on her mother's shoes and walking like her and claims that the wishful fantasy is immediately gratified although the result is transitory (Milrod, 2002, p. 134). Through this imitation, the self-representation experiences a sense of oneness with the object representation of the omnipotent mother and recovers some of the narcissistic satisfaction that was transferred upon the object representation.

Later in development, when the child's reality sense is more developed, fantasy surrounding the imitation of gestures, tones, or dress is not enough to satisfy the wish to achieve perfection. Thus, "selected admired qualities, abilities, or skills of idolized figures, which make up his aspirations and ambitions" Milrod writes, "become part of the … wished-for image" (ibid., p. 134). He notes that the child will work to attain the skill or quality with "surprising persistence" and the struggle to live up to the wished-for image resembles the struggle to live up to the standards of the ego ideal. However, there are some important differences between the two for Milrod. Firstly, the ego ideal only possesses moral or ethical standards. Secondly, although the skill may become the child's own it stems from an identification with a person while the "striving to approximate the values in the ego ideal, however, never leads to an identification" (ibid., p. 135). Instead, the child chooses his own values (instead of imitating an "idol") and constantly strives for his lofty ideals, but, at best, he only occasionally approximates them.

In parallel to the ego ideal, Milrod sees the pre-oedipal conscience as dependent on the parents. His banner for this position comes from a rather inexact statement of Freud's: "young children … possess no internal inhibitions against their impulses …. the part which is later taken on by the super-ego is played to begin with by an external power, by parental authority" (Freud, 1933, p. 62). Milrod holds that fear of parental retaliation is what holds a child in check before the guilt conscience. A child is simply seeking pleasure and avoiding pain. If the child hits a sibling, steals a cookie, or does something else a parent disapproves of, and which results in punishment, then the child becomes conditioned to associate a given act with pain or absence of pleasure. Milrod briefly acknowledges that other analysts have claimed earlier forms of conscience, such as Ferenczi's *sphincter morality*, but he claims that ego defences can explain them (Ferenczi, 1925). For example, early aggressive impulses towards parents or sibling can be "turned upon the self" and thus what appears as an unconscious need for punishment when an individual hurts or injures himself is the individual's own aggression directed at the self (Milrod, 2002, pp. 135–136).

The turn from the reliance upon particular individuals to self-reliance, and internalisation of the power of the parental figures after the Oedipus complex, is the most important moment in development for Milrod. Instead of the child inhibiting its behaviour due to fear of parental punishment, the individual's now independent conscience reacts to superego anxiety. This superego anxiety, issues from the "ideal values" that the child has selected for its ego ideal. Where before the child imitated particular people to varying degrees of complexity, after the Oedipus complex he or she strives to live up to "abstract, depersonalized standards" (ibid., p. 137). The ego ideal is comprised of admired moral ideals and conscience is comprised of "standards of unacceptable immoral and unethical behavior" that are linked to guilt feelings and self-punishment (ibid., p. 142). Recognising the "huge step" involved in this change, Milrod himself asks what it is that gives rise to this new found independence. He notes that there had been crises in development that occurred before Oedipus but he cites improved reality testing, reliance on reality gratification, and the function of language that have developed in the ego. Additionally, he claims that the parents are much less idealised by the Oedipus complex. "One parent is seen as castrated and the other as castrating" he writes, and this "creates a grand disillusionment" (ibid., p. 139). So, at a time when the child needs to rely on someone powerful he has no one to turn to, and this provides a tremendous stimulus to form the superego and be done with external dependence. Milrod claims that this change is to be understood in the mechanism of self-observation that moves from the ego to the superego. "The self-observing function of the ego concerns itself with every value other than morality" Milrod writes, and "with the resolution of the Oedipus complex, self observation becomes, in addition, a part of the superego" (ibid., p. 142). Thus, the autonomous, conflict-free zone in which the child chooses its values exists in the self-observation of the new superego agency.

It may seem provocative, if not foolish, to link ego psychologists with Lacanians in order to argue for a different interpretation of Freud's superego. However, one of Freud's most enduring observations has been "the narcissism of minor differences" in which people or groups that are very similar despise one another (Freud, 1930, p. 114). Noting the unending polemics that Lacanians make against the ego psychologists and the ego psychologists' cries of Lacan's unintelligibility, it is clear that they offend each other's vanity. I believe the similarity is showcased in their conceptualisation of the ego ideal and superego in general.

Lacanians have the preoedipal "ideal ego" that they differentiate from the oedipal ego ideal, while ego psychologists have the wished for self-image and imitative identifications that they conceive of as a "super-ego forerunner". Before the Oedipus complex, Lacanians theorise the "desire of the mother" and the child's attempt to fill the mother's lack or be or possess her missing phallus (Fink, 1995, pp. 54–55). This all-consuming project is replaced by the paternal phallus, the father as the law, the paternal metaphor, the name of the father, the unary trace, the master signifier, laws of the symbolic order, or the ego ideal depending, of course, on what phase of Lacan one adheres to or which Lacanian one reads and whether they deign to use Freudian terms. Fink indicates that "in accordance with Lacan's later usage, the Name-of-the-Father thus seems to be correlated with S, the master signifier" (ibid., p. 75). However, where the master signifier is related to the classical concept of "word-presentations" related to symptoms in the clinical realm, in the social realm the Oedipus complex and the overcoming of the ideal ego is, as with ego psychology, linked to moral values. The symbolic order or "'Other' with a capital 'O'", Fink (1997) writes, "generally refers to a person or institution serving a symbolic function (legislating, prohibiting, putting forward ideals, and so on)" (Fink, 1997, p. 232). Compared to the jouissance or narcissistic triumph of being the mother's desire, in the symbolic order, one desires through the ideals of the Other in a way that is never satisfied. Another Lacanian writes, "the identification with *symbolic laws* enables the subject to become free of the captivity of the imaginary and the narcissism of the ideal ego and of having to seek for the object in the imaginary field" (Moncayo, 2006, p. 587, emphasis mine). Žižek (2006), Lacan's most famous interpreter, writes:

> Lacan introduces a precise distinction between these three terms: the "ideal ego" stands for the idealized self-image of the subject (the way I would like to be, I would like others to see me); the Ego-Ideal is the agency whose gaze I try to impress with my ego image, the big Other who watches over me and propels me to give my best, the ideal I try to follow and actualize ... For Lacan, the seemingly benevolent agency of the Ego-Ideal which leads us to *moral growth and maturity*, forces us to betray the "law of desire" by way of adopting the "reasonable" demands of the existing socio-symbolic order. (Žižek, 2006, p. 45, emphasis mine)

All of these statements invite comparison to the ego psychological position. Take, for example, Loewald's comments:

> I have viewed the question of the centrality of the Oedipus complex and oedipal conflict as a version of and a specifically psychoanalytic focus on a fundamental human problem—the initiation of the child into an adult world, into the moral order, in short, into becoming an individual ... unless the oedipal level of his psychic life is available to the patient and he comes to understand it as a genuine step in his human development and not as a tragic decline from a state of grace, he remains a victim of the selfobject stage and its narcissism. (Loewald, 1985, pp. 440–442)

With the language of "moral maturation", "ideals of the symbolic order", and escaping the captivity of the "imaginary" or "ideal ego" it seems to me that Lacanians and ego psychologists are saying the same thing but with a different emphasis, or with the Lacanians providing a more clever formulation. For example, the wished for self-image that begins with the child aspiring to take on certain abilities or skills is not related to identification with a person directly, for Lacanians, but rather it is an identification with a signifier, given to the child by the mother. I believe they would say that the child doesn't form a cathexis to what it understands to be the meaning of being a painter or doing a painting, being a doctor, or whatever the mother's desire is. Instead the signifier, or acoustic-image of the word, is what is important. The signifier will take on different content or meaning later in life as the child's intelligence develops. Secondly, after the Oedipus complex the ego psychologists hold that the child "autonomously" chooses values, but the Lacanians place emphasis on the *de-centered subject*. They wouldn't see the child as choosing values but, as a modified form of structuralism, would see the individual inscribed with values through the symbolic order. However, whether values are rationally chosen by the individual or inscribed by the big Other, ideas or signifiers of moral values govern the individual.

Of course thinkers on both side of this divide transcend it. Loewald (1985), for example, writes of "responsibility to oneself within the context of authoritative norms consciously and *unconsciously* accepted or assimilated from parental and societal sources" as the "essence of the superego" (Loewald, 1985, p. 760, emphasis mine). Thinkers in both groups direct us to a narcissistic dimension of the ego ideal that, *contra* Milrod, is more than just ethical values. The problem is that the jargon involved doesn't stick close enough to phenomenology nor does it become operationalised in specific behaviour. I will show that Freud's work has some subtle distinctions that provide a chance to understand the blending of narcissistic and ethical elements associated with the ego ideal. However, for the moment, I would like to point out that without jargon we can very simply observe that a person is embedded in social relations and that after betrayals or disappointments in his love life or in the need to keep his work-life or his "good name" intact he may make promises to others or himself. I've had narcissistic patients who had social anxiety about cheating on exams or breaking the law and afterwards promised themselves they wouldn't do it again and stuck to it. I've also had similar patients promise themselves they would never be vulnerable in love or trust someone with their secrets. However, the ability to make promises to oneself or another is not specifically moral and one can also promise a vendetta or give "ones's word" or make "an oath" towards immoral ends too.

II

For Freud (1930), the later development of the conscience into the guilt conscience is the first time that feeling badly occurs from a reflection upon intentions rather than actions (p. 131). Additionally, reflection upon immoral actions is attached to a need to "come clean" and confess that isn't attached to the fear that an authority figure may find out about one's sins or misdeeds. *Contra* Milrod's interpretation, the guilt conscience is actually a post-oedipal development for Freud. "Social anxiety" that sees the individual merely seeking to avoid a reputation of immorality, is in fact, aligned with the Oedipus complex. The distinctive feature of the guilt conscience—the "self-observation" in which one feels oneself to be bad for having done, or having intended to do, something wrong—is used by Freud as a template for earlier forms of the superego and psychopathology. For example, Freud (1914a) cites "delusions of being watched" in which:

> patients ... complain that all their thoughts are known and their actions watched and supervised ... [as an illustration] of the functioning of this agency by voices which characteristically speak to them in the third person ("Now she's thinking of that again", "now he's going out"). (Freud, 1914a, p. 95)

I don't have the space to investigate the nature of the pre-oedipal superego in this chapter. I will say a little about it in the conclusion but save the majority of the discussion for the next chapter. Here I will only show that Freud sees a continuous line of development from the pre-oedipal to the post-oedipal forms of the superego in several places in his work. Additionally, I'll show that the attribution of self-observing functions to the ego by Milrod, *et al.*, is at odds with Freud's reasons for positing a superego: the tension that can exist between the ego and the self-observation is the very reason that Freud established it as a separate agency.

Milrod (2002) gives an example of superego guilt in the case of a married man who had an affair. His patient reported feelings of envy and lust regarding the actors he worked with as well as inferiority about his own appearance. He found a mature mistress who would understand the transitory and discrete nature of the relationship. His wife would never need to know of the affair and no one would be hurt in his estimation. He felt elated by the experience but when he got home his wife wasn't there and he was "thrust into morbid self-condemnation, and [was] certain his wife had learned of his adventure" (Milrod, 2002, p. 144). He called his wife's friends and family in desperation and he went to the bedroom in tears to escape in sleep. However, he found his wife and child asleep in the bed "like angels". Milrod writes that not finding his wife and imagining that she knew and had left him was a "punitive function of his superego indicating that he felt he deserved to be abandoned for his sin" and that his elation on the way home was "caused by denial of guilt feelings" (ibid., p. 144). This example highlights one of the many departures from the Freudian notion of the superego in Milrod's work. Milrod's representation of the philanderer's guilt emphasises fear of an external authority, his wife, more than the internal sense that adultery and deception are wrong.

In his most sustained investigation of the superego in *Civilization and Its Discontents*, Freud (1930) writes:

> to begin with, if we ask how a person comes to have a sense of guilt, we arrive at an answer which cannot be disputed: a person feels guilty (devout people would say "sinful") when he has done something which he knows to be "bad" … we shall add that even when a person has not actually done the bad thing but has only recognized in himself an intention to do it, he may regard himself as guilty; and the question then arises of why the intention is regarded as equal to the deed. (Freud, 1930, p. 124)

In this quotation Freud observes that guilt is a feeling that can be felt after having committed a bad action but also that one can feel guilt after merely entertaining the intention to do something that is "wrong". A man, for example, can have sexual thoughts about his wife's sister and then feel bad about entertaining plans to have some time alone with her. The view of himself as someone who would contemptibly violate his marriage vows results in guilt. Additionally, we all know people who do something wrong, and aren't found out, but yet have to confess to their spouses or whoever they wrong in order to be square with their conscience. A superego conscience *qua* guilt means that someone will seek the forgiveness of the other for his "trespasses" even in the face of potential punishment or bad consequences for his actions, and not because he believes he will be found out. Milrod's case reads as a study in the avoidance of punishment and shows none of the earmarks of guilt. His patient never brought up reservations about his affair before he had it—when it was just an intention—and there is no discussion of a confession to his wife afterwards. What

Milrod describes has much more in common with what Freud calls "social anxiety":

> this state of mind is called a "bad conscience"; but actually it does not deserve this name, for at this stage the sense of guilt is clearly only a fear of loss of love, "social" anxiety. In small children it can never be anything else, but in many adults, too, it has only changed to the extent that the place of the father or the two parents is taken by the larger human community. Consequently, such people habitually allow themselves to do any bad thing which promises them enjoyment, so long as they are sure that the authority will not know anything about it or cannot blame them for it; they are afraid only of being found out. (Freud, 1930, pp. 124–125)

While Milrod casually uses the term "social anxiety" to refer to the pre-oedipal form of conscience, Freud designates it as the direct outcome of the Oedipus complex (Freud, 1914b, p. 102; 1926a, p. 139). While the guilt conscience involves the ability to feel guilt about one's intentions (without having performed the deed) social anxiety is a state in which one can entertain bad intentions without guilt and perform them without scruple so long as one isn't found out. For Milrod's patient to not have had any reservations before the deed, to not seek to come clean after, and for him to impute knowledge of the event to his wife though he was no doubt very careful to conceal things from her shows a child-like overestimation of her as an authority and locus of right and wrong. His worry and desperate feelings match the description of social anxiety much better than the guilt conscience. In order to call his reaction guilt Milrod (2002) has to claim several defences before and after the fact to explain his behaviour (p. 144). Moreover, if the patient felt like he had to tell his wife and come clean after he and Milrod worked through his defences, I'm not sure why Milrod would leave this out of the account.

Now that we have a functional understanding of how the guilty person acts and have seen that Freud links social anxiety and not the guilt conscience to the Oedipus complex, I'd like to begin to outline an alternate interpretation of Freud's superego. In section IV and V I will examine the specifics about how oedipal social anxiety develops into the post-oedipal guilt conscience. For now, I'd like to turn to Freud's texts in order to show that, although there are passages in which it appears that he claims the superego is formed from the Oedipus complex, there are also many statements to the opposite effect.

The very inexact statements Freud makes about the child initially having no conscience and only fearing parental authority, I take to be hyperbolic in order to stress the fact that many people lack the *guilt* conscience in the way just described. "As regards conscience", Freud (1933) writes, "God has done an uneven and careless piece of work, for a large majority of men have brought along with them only a modest amount of it or scarcely enough to be worth mentioning" (Freud, 1933, p. 61). It is to establish the phenomenological/characterological coordinates to judge the guilt conscience that Freud stresses the post-oedipal superego. Its value is for the clinician and not because of some sense of freedom or autonomy that Freud occasionally uses the superego as synonym for guilt conscience. The child who doesn't resolve the post-oedipal stage to form the guilt conscience still has a superego. However, "the super-ego is stunted in its strength and growth if the surmounting of the Oedipus complex is only incompletely successful" in Freud's account (Freud, 1933, p. 64). In *Civilization and Its Discontents* Freud (1930) formulates this explicitly:

> a great change takes place only when the authority is internalized through the establishment of a super-ego. The phenomena of conscience then reach a higher stage. Actually, it is not until now that we should speak of conscience or a sense of guilt. (Freud, 1930, p. 125)

Freud's sensitivity is to the use of the word "conscience" in the phenomenological form that is attached to guilt: feeling bad about one's "sins" or sinful intentions; and feeling the need to confess. Common language makes important distinctions between words. People with wisdom or good judgement are able to employ words to get at specific types of motivations, emotions, or feelings. A person who lacks good judgement may use guilt in order to speak about every type of reaction of conscience but Freud wishes to use it for one type. Similarly a person without good judgement may simply say another person looks scared while wisdom will allow another observer to differentiate the other's mien and behaviour in order to say they are spooked, horrified, shocked, terrified, timid, etc. As I pointed out last chapter, Freud explicitly points to common language as directing the inquiry into ego psychology and the dependence of the depths of the mind on judging the surface (Freud, 1926b, p. 195; 1933, p. 60). Following Freud's concern I will only use guilt to denote the reaction of someone who has developed the post-oedipal conscience that has been described. However, I will continue to use conscience for the prohibitive aspect of the super-ego and bad conscience to denote the punitive reactions of the super-ego to prohibited actions even though they are feelings that only arise after the deed has been done. Following the quotation from *Civilization* above, Freud (1930) provides a footnote that explicitly takes the position that the conscience existed before and had developed:

> everyone of discernment will understand and take into account the fact that in this summary description we have sharply delimited events which in reality occur by gradual transitions, and that it is not merely a question of the existence of a super-ego but of its relative strength and sphere of influence. (Freud, 1930, p. 125)

In admitting that there are gradual transitions and that it is a question of relative strength and influence, Freud reveals that he stresses the sphere of influence and strength of the post-oedipal superego for didactic reasons. The active-egoistic individual who hasn't made the instinctual renunciations to form the post-oedipal guilt conscience is what we call "self-absorbed." He only cares about his own success or passionate love. He will lie and cheat if he believes he will get ahead by it and doesn't feel the claims of justice or fairness to be normative. Freud (1916) has described such individuals as "the exceptions" and in an earlier piece writes:

> civilization is built up on the suppression of instincts. Each individual has sundered some part of his assets—some part of the sense of omnipotence or of the aggressive or vindictive inclinations in his personality. From, these contributions has grown civilization's common assets in material and ideal wealth ... The man who, in consequence of his unyielding constitution, cannot fall in with this suppression of instinct, becomes a "criminal", an "outlaw" in the face of society—unless his social position or his exceptional capacities enable him to impose himself upon it as a great man, a "hero". (Freud, 1908, pp. 186–187)

Although this passage is relatively early in Freud's writings, the temptation to lie and cheat in order to attain success and be "loved by fate" and the idea that some people never acquire a guilt conscience exists to the end of Freud's work (Freud, 1930, pp. 126–127; 1933, p. 64). Thus, it seems that Kohut's famous dichotomy of the "tragic man" and the "guilty man" was already acknowledged in Freud's system (Kohut, 1977). Additionally, the motivation of personal happiness is absolutely foundational in Adler's individual psychology and Freud's continuing references to Adler's "masculine protest" show that he was sympathetic to the view that:

> all failures—neurotics, psychotics, criminals, drunkards, problem children, suicides, perverts, and prostitutes—are failures because they are lacking in social interest ... Their goal of success is a *goal of personal superiority, and their triumphs have meaning only to themselves*. (Adler, 1946, p. 156, emphasis mine)

Self-absorption and the goals of personal happiness leave the subject egoist dependent upon finding success and passionate love. When they aren't forthcoming it can lead to an attack on the community that frustrates him or upon himself or his sexual object. However, as I showed in the last chapter, *contra* Adler, Freud recognises that passive-altruistic drives are also central and that personal superiority isn't the whole story. I will continue to investigate the pre-guilt conscience striving for happiness of the subject egoist in the next section but for now I'll return to the pre-oedipal development of the superego.

In the last section I mentioned that Milrod's position on conscience has been based upon inexact passages from Freud's *New Introductory Lectures*. Milrod (2002) writes:

> it is important to be aware that morality does not begin with the formation of the superego. In fact morality helps guide behavior even in the preoedipal period. But this kind of morality is entirely different since it is largely influenced by external authorities and their dictates of right and wrong. Freud said something similar when he wrote, "Young children ... possess no internal inhibitions against their impulses .... The part which is later taken on by the super-ego is played to begin with by an external power, by parental authority". (Milrod, 2002, pp. 136–137)

There are a number of problems with this quotation. First, Freud writes that although sexuality exists from the "beginning of life" conscience does not, but he only mentions general "parental authority" and not parental authority at the Oedipus complex. When he does bring up the Oedipus complex he explicitly claims that "this new creation of a superior agency within the ego is most intimately linked with the destiny of the Oedipus complex" (Freud, 1933, p. 64). The elliptical nature of this phrasing suggests an indistinct relationship in time between the creation of the "superior agency" and the experience of the Oedipus complex.

Later in this passage in *The New Introductory Lectures* Freud (1933) is explicit that the superego has been developing before this. Although it's not there at "the beginning of life" and initially prohibitions aren't internal, it does begin its development at some point prior to the Oedipus complex:

> a child has a different estimate of its parents at different periods of its life. At the time at which the Oedipus complex gives place to the super-ego they are something quite magnificent; but later they lose much of this. Identifications then come about with these later parents as well, and indeed they regularly make important contributions to the formation of character; *but in that case they only affect the ego, they no longer influence the super-ego, which has been determined by the earliest parental imagos.* (Freud, 1933, p. 64, emphasis mine)

I'm going to wait until the next section before I get into details about the status of the parental imago in Freud's work. Suffice it to say, for the moment, that Freud explicitly claims there are multiple imagos that form a phase-specific "estimation" or perception of the parents/ authority figures and that they "determine" the superego. Even though there are many other passages about the superego existing throughout development, and many more when Freud was using ego ideal to refer to the agency, I can't shake the feeling that interpreters of Freud believe there is a single form of the superego because Freud refers to the agency superego in the singular. However, Freud also refers to the agency of the Id as singular but people will acknowledge that it holds many different aggressive and affectionate drives (Freud, 1933, p. 120). Additionally, Freud (1923b) refers to the ego in the singular but also describes it as "precipitate of abandoned object cathexes" that are related to multiple ego and object drives (p. 29). When Freud isn't stressing the importance of the guilt conscience as a phenomenological coordinate and is speaking generally of development he clearly sees the superego as existing throughout development:

> the effects of the first identifications made in earliest childhood will be general and lasting. This leads us back to the origin of the ego ideal [superego]; for behind it there lies hidden an individual's first and most important identification, his identification with the father in his own personal prehistory. (Freud, 1923b, p. 31)
>
> The super-ego is, however, not simply a residue of the earliest object-choices of the id; it also represents.... (Freud, 1923b, p. 34)
>
> The super-ego arises, as we know, from an identification with the father taken as a model. *Every such* identification is in the nature of a desexualization or even of a sublimation. (Freud, 1923b, p. 54, emphasis mine)
>
> The libidinal trends belonging to the Oedipus complex are in part desexualized and sublimated (*a thing which probably happens with every transformation into an identification*) and in part inhibited in their aim and changed into impulses of affection. (Freud, 1924a, pp. 176–177, emphasis mine)

While many analysts recognise that the cognition of the child advances as the ego is derived from id, Freud is clear that the superego is around very early in the child's development. Freud's explicit position in *The Ego and the Id* is that:

> the ego is formed to a great extent out of identifications which take the place of abandoned cathexes by the id; [and] that the first of these identifications always behave as a special agency in the ego and stand apart from the ego in the form of a super-ego. (Freud, 1923b, p. 48)

In none of these passages does Freud claim that the superego he is writing about is merely a "superego forerunner" and something separate from the post-oedipal guilt conscience version. Again, the guilt conscience appears to be used as a synonym for the superego to the extent that its lack in people is of supreme clinical relevance. In "Libidinal types", for example, Freud (1931b) bases the obsessional (one of three types!) on people "dominated by fear of their conscience" and contrasted it to the preceding narcissistic type who, on the surface, appears to have "no tension between ego and super-ego" (Freud, 1931b, p. 218).

Freud argues for the earlier existence of the superego on more than just an admission that there must be some kind of development of the conscience aspect of the superego before it becomes the guilt conscience. Although he doesn't give us examples of the pre-oedipal forms of conscience he does argue that the guilt conscience self-observation has been an ongoing "structural relation and is not merely a personification of some such abstraction as that of conscience" (Freud, 1933, p. 64). Freud links the self-observation of the guilt conscience to psychopathology of earlier stages. As I quoted in the beginning of this section paranoid delusions of being watched were taken to be a truth of the internal world that was externalised and illustrated pre-oedipal "self-observation" which necessitates a grade in the ego. This grade in the ego is an over-ego or agency that can take the ego as an object and Freud soon famously went on to add melancholia as another example of this phenomenon. In *Group Psychology* Freud (1921) held that investigation in the psychoses would yield more material on the superego (still the ego ideal at this time):

> the assumption of this kind of *differentiating grade in the ego* as a first step in an analysis of the ego must gradually establish its justification in the most various regions of psychology. In my paper on narcissism I have put together all the pathological material that could at the moment be used in support of this differentiation. But it may be expected that *when we penetrate deeper into the psychology of the psychoses its significance will be discovered to be far greater*. Let us reflect that *the ego now enters into the relation of an object to the ego ideal* which has been developed out of it, and that all the interplay between an external object and the ego as a whole, with which our study of the neuroses has made us acquainted, *may possibly be repeated upon this new scene of action within the ego*. (Freud, 1921, p. 130, emphasis mine)

The examples of psychopathology and Freud's hope that analysis of the psychoses would yield more to say about the pre-oedipal superego illustrates that self-observation doesn't magically appear with the guilt conscience from some increase of cognition at the Oedipus complex. Rather, it is a relation between the internalised image of the parents (imagos) that form the superego and the ego *qua* drive agency throughout development. Although the superego is represented in the singular as an agency it is determined by multiples imagos and it is the sum of the relations of each imago with each of their potential tensions: their melancholic self-punishments and paranoid ideations in pathology; as well as the potential feelings of inferiority, guilt, etc. when the ego is perceived as not fulfilling the standards of the imago. "Each of the mental differentiations that we have become acquainted with represents a fresh aggravation of the difficulties of mental functioning" Freud writes, every grade in the ego "increases its instability, and may become the starting-point for its breakdown, that is, for the onset of a disease" (ibid., p. 130).

Milrod, and Hartmann before him, represent the Oedipus complex as creating a singular superego agency. Milrod (2002) also writes of the ego providing "self-directed criticism or punishment ... in the preoedipal period" and possessing the self-observation function which Freud has identified with the superego (ego ideal), as a grade in the ego (p. 137). In order to support this view Milrod claims that though Freud initially posited self-observation in the superego he moved it to the ego and then moved it back to the superego again in the *New Introductory Lectures* (Milrod, 2002, p. 142). However, Freud only moved "reality-testing" from the superego back to the ego and never moved self-observation from the superego. Again, Freud's definition of the superego is that it is self-consciousness or self-observational and requires a "grade in the ego" or a "nucleus" that is different than the ego and can come into conflict with it (Freud, 1927b, p. 164; 1933, pp. 59–60).

I understand Milrod and Hartmann to make this claim in order to give support to their interpretation of the post-oedipal superego as representing a new autonomy. The superego's post-oedipal self-observation is contrasted with the pre-oedipal ego's self-observation and the former now becomes a conflict-free zone in which the individual is now able to rationally choose what values he or she wants. I'll evaluate this claim based upon its own merits or flaws in section IV, but for the moment I have only been concerned with showing that it is not Freud's position. Since the superego autonomy that ego psychologists claims isn't found in Freud I'll attempt to show in the next section that it's likely source is as a refinement of the popular "rational chooser" or Cartesian model of freedom that marks our Modern Western tradition. In order to do so, I'm going to shift the focus from the conscience to the ego ideal aspect of the superego in order explain the concept of the imago and how Freud's conflict model opposes the Cartesian view. Then in sections IV and V I'll go on to show that Freud's model still opposes the ego psychology refinement of this position and gives a superior formulation in that Freud makes historical arguments to back up his claims.

III

The superego is almost fully identified with its prohibitory or conscience function in popular understanding. However, along with the prohibitory and punitive function the superego also has a "direction-giving" aspect in which the phase specific parental image of perfection "demands perfection" from the ego (Freud, 1914b, p. 94; 1923b, p. 34; 1933, p. 65). The ego ideal measures the performance of the ego and object drives so that the subject egoist experiences triumph in social or romantic success or feels self-contempt or inferiority in failure. The pre-oedipal forms of perfection are the subject of the next chapter. In this section I investigate the way the ego ideal is linked to the father imago of the Oedipus complex and has what Freud (1921) calls "a double kind of tie" in which self-esteem is regulated by the father imago through "father-substitutes" who guide one through maturation. This view of maturation is inspired by the work of Chasseguet-Smirgel who argues that along with the "difference between the sexes", the Oedipus complex also establishes the "difference between the generations" that sees the child recognise the superiority of the father's potency (Chasseguet-Smirgel, 1976a, p. 282; Chasseguet-Smirgel, 1976b, p. 354, 358). The father imago mediates relations with those who have more Prestige in one's community or are recognised by the individual as having superior skills or intelligence in a certain field. Freud also indicates that the ego-istic individual can detach from, or no long respect, father-substitutes and that this amounts to the individual having the "single wish to be his own father" in the castration complex (Freud, 1910, p. 173).

In the last section I began by giving the phenomenological coordinates of how guilt operates and by criticising Milrod's account for being built on examples that better showcase social anxiety than guilt. We saw that Freud holds that the guilt conscience is an important characterological culmination of the superego but that the self-observation that occurred in the guilt conscience wasn't an achievement in cognition but existed earlier. Freud attached it to the superego-determining imagos or internalised images of the parents from different stages of development. In this section I get into more detail about Freud's concept of the imago and its relation to the ego ideal of the Oedipus complex. He uses the term imago in other ways that I won't investigate here. For example, imago is also used by Freud (1912) to explain the phenomenon of transference and the activation of traumatic fixation with the parents or siblings in one's childhood that becomes repeated (p. 102). A synonym of the term, "father-substitute", is also used to talk about symbols that are generated in myth and religion in way that is analogous to Jung's archetype (Freud, 1923a, p. 85).

In this chapter I'll only investigate the imago in its non-pathological and symbolic form. As I'll show the imago has a "depersonalised" aspect that comes to represent a segment of the community or what I've come to call the *social body*. This contrasts with the "personalised" side that imprints the masculine, feminine, or particular sensuous features of the actual parent onto parental substitutes in repetition-compulsions that don't follow the depersonalised relations. Instead of a mother-substitute being a woman of a higher class or who has more Prestige than him, for example, a subject egoist might end up with a woman who has his mother's eyes or resembles her physically in some way. Additionally, in my analytic work with narcissistic neuroses I've often met with patients who return to live with their parents and who regress to childish relationships with them that suggest that the personalised aspect of the imago allows them to once again see the childhood estimate of perfection in them.

The inter-relation of the ego and object drives and the imagos of the superego can be seen in the genesis of each. Firstly, the child forms an "id object-cathexis" or "erotic object choice" of its mother or mother's body that it "instinctually renounces" to form the ego and object drives that "press ever forward unsubdued" (Freud, 1920, p. 42; 1923b, pp. 29–30). In active-egoistic development the ego drives aim at "perfection", "magnification of the individual", "mastery", and Freud also compares them to Adler's "will to power" (Freud, 1917a, p. 137; 1924b, p. 163; 1933, p. 96). Then, after these ego and object drives are formed the child forsakes this striving to recognise the father's superior potency and forms a *primary identification* or permanent introjection that forms an imago (Freud, 1917b, p. 329; 1921, p. 105; 1923b, pp. 28–34).

This imago is seen in potential tensions between the superego and ego. For example, the ambitious individual who is driven to strive for the admiration of others and needs to have the reputation of belonging to the intelligent, skilled, or eminently competent class of people in their places of work, or in the community, will feel jealousy towards peers who he see as superior or have inferiority tensions if he does not accomplish goals that they do. Individuals *transfer* the authority, power, or perfection that they felt toward their fathers in childhood to individuals who are judged as superior or who occupy higher positions of authority in social hierarchy. A woman can receive transference in this way from a man and in the next chapter I argue that the father doesn't have natural superiority but rather that he, or his phallus, comes to symbolise the imago relation to those with more Prestige, skill, or knowledge because he represents the "not-mother" in binary logic.

At the Oedipus complex, the object or sexual relationship drives of the egoistic child are aim inhibited by the incest taboo. This results in an idealisation, of and affectionate feelings towards, the love object, where before sensuality and aggression was dominant over affection (Freud, 1921, p. 111). Preceding the Oedipus complex, the egoist wanted to posses or control the sexual object, or, his infatuation was over after he has sexual relations with the object—a position many egoists regress to. Freud also captures this love idealisation, which is longer-lasting than infatuation, in his formulation that the individual puts the beloved within his ego ideal (ibid., p. 113). The ego ideal also modifies the competitive ego drives. They become directed to certain goals in a work-group by taking a "father-substitute" who is similarly placed in the ego ideal (ibid., p. 116, 127). In "The Economic Problem of Masochism" Freud (1924b) describes this same process as being underpinned by the imagos of the parents. He writes that in "the Oedipus complex ... [the parent's] personal significance for the superego recedes into the background' and 'the imagos they leave behind ... link [to] the influences of teachers and authorities ..." (Freud, 1924b, pp. 167–168). Freud (1919a) also refers to this outcome of the Oedipus complex in other places: "the father persists in the shape of a teacher or some other person in authority ... a substitute taken from the class of fathers" (Freud, 1924b, p. 196, 190; 1910, p. 133).

As we saw last section, narcissists can escape social anxiety as long as "the authority will not know anything about [their bad behaviour] or cannot blame them for it" (Freud, 1930, p. 125). A "father-substitute", from the "class of fathers", can possess this power because he receives a transference from the individual because he or she is judged to be more knowledgeable, skilled, or wise than oneself or because he or she has a position of Prestige or authority in one's community, or culture at large, that indicates this. Freud writes:

> we can now understand our relation to our schoolmasters. These men, not all of whom were in fact fathers themselves, became our substitute fathers. That was why, even though they were still quite young, they struck us as so mature and so unattainably adult. We transferred on to them the respect and expectations attaching to the omniscient father of our childhood, and we then began to treat them as we treated our fathers at home. We confronted them with the ambivalence that we had acquired in our own families and with its help we struggled with them as we had been in the habit of struggling with our fathers ... (Freud, 1914c, p. 244)

In regard to someone whose self-esteem comes from egoism related to knowledge the dependency on oedipal father-substitutes and the ladder of maturation is straightforward. The subject-egoist wants power and to gain respect or admiration from others for his knowledge and he encounters father-substitutes in first school, then secondary school, college, university, (etc.). Even if he gets his PhD he may still transfer authority to those who went to more prestigious universities or have jobs at them. However, if he goes to the highest institutions or engaged enough with the work from people there to remain confident about his own abilities then Freud (1924b) holds that destiny becomes his father-substitute (pp. 167–168). If he has understood more knowledge than others and has been able to synthesise it into something new and original then it is his destiny to either have his contribution recognised and change the understanding in his field or, to die with his work unrecognised—though he may possibly be discovered later. Someone who is not competitive in relation to a field of knowledge will, by contrast, encounter father-substitutes in school, and may complete some college, but then later find his mentors in the business world. He will take his measure from the financial success of someone's business or from a father-substitute's membership to a certain country club or other such group that confers status. Learning certain ideas, and skills is certainly important here but also there is learning how to know the "right people", how to dress, and acquiring certain manners.

The question may arise as to how Freud can theorise this? Freud, following Alfred Adler, cites the inability for some patients to have an oedipal transference to the analyst. The masculine protest, as the social aspect of the castration complex, is called the "bedrock of analysis" and is cited by Freud (1937) into his last writings (p. 250). I have found Wilhelm Reich's work helpful to see the phenomenological manifestations of the castration complex in my patients. Reich gets into minute clinical detail about how such "patients are wont to ridicule every analytic effort" and hold themselves superior to the analyst (Reich, 1990, p. 123). However, again, this isn't merely with the analyst, but is the inability to take "subordinate positions in the rank and file" of worklife with father-substitutes (ibid., pp. 123, 217–218). So when someone is always smarter than his teachers or professors, critical with his bosses, or dismissive of his analyst, whether it is "cocky" and overt or more covert, then the person may be suspected as suffering from a masculine protest or castration complex.

Freud relates the ego ideal to the Oedipus complex father-imago by holding that the ego ideal possesses a "double kind of tie which this makes possible ... putting the object in the place of the ego ideal" (Freud, 1921, p. 130). So long as this double tie is in place the individual is on the path of acquiring Prestige in his community or culture. He gets his BA, for example, and then puts the professors of his post-graduate programme in his ego ideal and defers to their criticisms and is able to develop some comradery with his fellow graduate students because they too are under his father-substitutes. I've come to understand the placement of the father-substitute in the ego ideal as the best example of Freud's later use of "eros", or "fusion" of the drives. Freud holds that the "super-ego arises, as we know, from an identification with the father taken as a model ... [and that] defusion would be the source of the general character of harshness and cruelty exhibited by the ideal—its dictatorial 'Thou shalt'" (Freud, 1923b, pp. 54–55). When the father-substitute is in the subject egoist's ego ideal, or he is in fusion with the father-imago, he doesn't feel the inferiority tensions and has respect for authority and trust that he will mature and eventually take the father's place. In defusion, the individual doesn't trust in the father-substitute and feels compelled to be admired like, or become, his own father.

Representations of this defusion differ. The subject egoist may deceptively present himself to others as having the potential to be greater than father-substitutes. By impressing others and trying to have them believe he is powerful he is able to believe it himself, but secretly fears being unmasked as a fraud (McDougall, 1974). Additionally, he may actually be driven to actual social achievements to prove his superiority as Reich and Fenichel document (Reich, 1990, p. 180; Fenichel, 1938, p. 431). Generally, the individual regards himself—his knowledge, skill, or wisdom—as superior to those who have more Prestige or social authority. He becomes competitive with his cohort or others in the work-group and no longer able to admire their skill and "put the work first". Defusion of the ego ideal means that the individual loses his regulated supply of self-esteem (narcissistic libido). The ego ideal that loses its "double tie" to a father-substitute and becomes an individual ego ideal that is suffused with inferiority no matter how well it's concealed (Reich, 1990, p. 23, 81, 180).

Although they don't avail themselves of Freud's formulation of the superego providing a connection to authority figures, this position has been put forward in many ways. Along with the true self and false self notions of some analysts, Wilhelm Reich, on the side of the drive, and Fairbairn, on the side of object relations, both acknowledge the difference between self-esteem that is regulated with whole objects and secondary or pathological relations that appear from frustration. Reich notes this in his difference between "primary" and "secondary drives", while Fairbairn notes it in his distinction between the object seeking "reality-principle" and the impulses of the "pleasure-principle" (Reich, 1990, p. 161, 207, 513; Fairbairn, 1952, p. 89).

Like the self-observation of the guilt conscience, Freud doesn't see this double tie, which allows an individual to put a father-substitute in place of the ego ideal, as an attribute of developed cognition. Rather, he sees it as part of the nature of social animals, which in the next chapter I refer to as social ontology. The mind develops from frustration of aggressive and affectionate impulses that are ended by "instinctual renunciation" that create drives that are in turn followed by "primary identifications" to form imagos. Freud attributes this same process to animals and sees "organic repression" leading to identification and a superego in animals as well (Freud, 1930, p. 103, 105). Freud explicitly states that higher animals possess a superego and uses the wolf pack with its alpha as an example of group psychology (Paskauskas, 1993, p. 461). "A superego" he writes, "must be presumed to be present wherever, as is the case with man, there is a long period of dependence in childhood" (Freud, 1938, p. 147). This means that depersonalisation doesn't just occur at the Oedipus complex but that it occurs with earlier imagos and will provide an input for group psychology and coordinates for the measurement of perfection. Again, it's not dependent on language or advanced cognition, but upon the social animal nature of humans; although language, as a tool, can communicate how we are measured in relation to the group. I will have some more to say about this in the conclusion and it will be investigated in detail in the next chapter.

As with the guilt conscience, Freud doesn't offer examples of the pre-oedipal ego ideal. Instead, what he offers is a general theory of a characterological "economy of libido" in which the parental imagos are "superordinate agencies" paired with ego and object drives as "subordinate agencies" to give individuals a characteristic way of striving for happiness. In the introduction I quoted a long passage on the characterological economy of the libido in which Freud discusses the man of action, the narcissistic man, and the erotic man in a brief sketch of phenomenological differences (Freud, 1930, pp. 83–84). In doing so, Freud privileges desire over decision-making. A person doesn't consciously choose what turns him or her on sexually. It is based upon their psychosexual development. In parallel, a child doesn't choose to derive its self-esteem (narcissism) from competing with and outshining others, from receiving approval for being loyal and devoted to another, or from being regarded as being attractive and desirable to others. In this parallel psycho-social development, the drive to be regarded as desirable to others, for example, can have an economic significance for the individual over the other drives because the child has formed a "high ego ideal" at a certain stage in relation to this drive, or, because he has defended against the other drives, or from other fluctuations in his economy of libido.[2] This ideal doesn't have to do with any objective assessment of how handsome he is, for example, and there are some attractive people who don't gain self-esteem from compliments or the admiration they receive for their beauty. In regard to both one's social [ego] approach to the world and one's approach to sexual [object] relationships Freud holds that

> psycho-analysis has taught us that the individual's emotional attitudes to other people, which are of such extreme importance

to his later behaviour, are already established at an unexpectedly early age. The nature and quality of the human child's relations to people of his own and the opposite sex have already been laid down in the first six years of his life. He may afterwards develop and transform them in certain directions, but he can no longer get rid of them ... These substitute figures can be classified from his point of view according as they are derived from what we call the "imagos" of his father, his mother, his brothers and sisters, and so on. His later acquaintances are thus obliged to take over a kind of emotional heritage; they encounter sympathies and antipathies to the production of which they themselves have contributed little. (Freud, 1914c, p. 243)

Based upon psychosexual and psycho-social development, the different ways a person strives for happiness in his public and private life are determined by imagos. A person doesn't decide he wants to go after success and power but instead he is "driven" to do so. He will experience a tension (for example, inferiority, self-contempt, etc.) between his ego and ego ideal demand for perfection based upon the estimate or image of perfection drawn from the parental imago he identified with. This model of being driven by parental imagos is a "Copernican revolution" of the popular Western or Cartesian tradition of seeing the ego as master in its own house. In this model the individual is a rational chooser who decides for himself whether he will work hard or not, or ambitiously strive for glory and is, therefore, responsible for his poverty if he doesn't. It also involves a mind-body split in which logic and rational decision-making is our human essence and our animal bodies are filled with passions that can cloud our decision-making. However, instead of seeing the mind as unitary and saying mental illness is due to a chemical imbalance or something wrong with the physical brain or body, Freud takes mental illness to show that the mind is made up of parts (imagos and drives). The splits in the pathological mind exist in the normal mind but appear as whole because of the "fusion" of drives with the superego:

if we throw a crystal to the floor, it breaks; but not into haphazard pieces. It comes apart along its lines of cleavage into fragments whose boundaries, though they were invisible, were predetermined by the crystal's structure. Mental patients are split and broken structures of this same kind. Even we cannot withhold from them something of the reverential awe which peoples of the past felt for the insane. They have turned away from external reality, but for that very reason they know more about internal, psychical reality and can reveal a number of things to us that would otherwise be inaccessible to us. (Freud, 1917b, p. 58)

The Cartesian or popular Western view claims that the mind must be whole or "indivisible" and cannot account for the breaks of the mind in mental illness except to say that something has gone wrong with the body or one's chemicals. In the Cartesian model a person simply decides to be ambitious or not, and some internal conflict free zone that is "the self" or ego in control is posited. However, as Nietzsche points out, it's not as if one gets to choose what ideas come to mind. An idea comes to mind when "it" wants, and so we have no direct access to what determines our ideas and therefore what we "will" or decide to do or not (Nietzsche, 2000, p. 17).[3] The Cartesian model doesn't have an empirical footing but, by accounting for breaks in the mind and the rigid behaviour of different complexes that manifest in different individuals in a similar way, Freud bases his model on empirical observation. Freud, like Copernicus, takes the earth/ego out of the centre and replaces it with the sun/imagos in order to account for functional patterns. The Cartesians simply claim that there is a will even though there is no subjective proof for it, while Freud provides a place for dreams, slips, and the broken mind to argue that the allegedly simple "will [is] directed by the reports" from his "hierarchy of superordinated and subordinated agencies" (Freud, 1917a, p. 141). In Freud's view the will may appear simple on the surface, or for consciousness, but in itself is determined by, or must satisfy, many different and often conflicting agencies. There may be an argument that an individual does have freedom in whether he remains fused to the father imago or chooses to become his own father. Additionally, since Freud (1923b) holds the father imago can have a good or bad aspect then re-fusion with the bad father imago might also approximate an individual choosing to be evil—but I will leave this for the philosophers to decide.

The superego autonomy that ego psychologists claim for Freud is not found in Freud's writings. A likely source for this idea is the popular "rational chooser" or Cartesian model of freedom that marks our Modern Western tradition. I understand Milrod, as with many, but not all ego psychologists, to want to leave Freud's conflict model. Notably, Brenner (1994) has divided the camp but the initial thrust from Hartmann has continued to find adherents as Milrod's work illustrates. Those that leave the conflict model offer a refinement of the Cartesian position by claiming that although what drives us to happiness can't be chosen, the will does become an expression of the rational self at some point in development. The pre-oedipal mind is in conflict, and even though one can regress to it, when one is normal (not regressed), one has chosen, and holds oneself to, certain values and principles.

In Milrod's account the pre-oedipal conflict is formalised in his claim that the ego has self-observation. The centrality of the Oedipus complex, as the point of defusion from the father imago is replaced by the pre-oedipal "wished-for self image" that is put on an "idolized leader" (Milrod, 1990, p. 56). However, this misses the subsequent defused castration complex from which "disappointment over a woman" (object drives) or "a mishap in social relations with other men" (ego drives) is the cause of regression or symptom formation (Freud, 1911b, p. 62). Although there are still important dynamics that need to be understood in this process, such as the role of the "need for punishment" in the symptom formation that Freud added later, my interest in this chapter is to show the divergences of Freud's structural model from the ego psychological one—not to comprehensively detail the causation of neurosis.

IV

Freud holds that oedipal social anxiety develops into the first form of the guilt conscience in the following father complex, and in latency it undergoes further transformations. In the father complex Freud explicitly bases the guilt conscience on the father imago that comes to function like Kant's *categorical imperative*. However, instead of an action being permissible because it doesn't form a logical contradiction if all others acted on it, a simpler account of the "Talion rule" or "an eye for an eye ..." is constructed following the behaviour of the imago in symptoms. Guilt emerges when an action the causes someone else pain or anxiety is phantasied to be performed upon oneself in return.

In order to reconcile a contradictory statement of Freud's—that the guilt conscience is formed on "social prototypes"—I add the qualification that although the imago provides the value through the Talion rule, the ideas about who is considered a legitimate citizen or person in one's community affect who is placed in the imago (or object) relation (Freud, 1926a, p. 139). This means that although morality is trans-historical that it, like marriage, doesn't treat certain groups of people as equals or peers. In the further development of the latency guilt conscience the child doesn't overcome dependence, but instead dependence on parental-substitutes moves to dependence on identity and tradition. In contrast, Milrod's position blends these different developments together and is therefore an ahistorical account that examines the individual from the contemporary standpoint of globalisation. In primitive political-economies that lack the texts and formalised principles of different world-views and religions, different characterological types will still be found. Therefore Milrod's account captures something closer to ration-alisation of one's libidinal economy. Freud recognises that morality, along with the incest taboo/marriage and religion are not introduced based upon rational arguments but because of the psychology of the imago. When "social prototypes" influence the superego it is through dependency on "social reality" (i.e., classes, traditions, etc.) and not the notion of the child internalising reality "in itself" and choosing values to bridge a primarily separate or atomistic condition.

Freud's writings about the post-oedipal superego are remarkably complex and, as I've already shown, he holds that the Oedipus complex is associated with the parental imago being depersonalised into social anxiety. This means the guilt conscience must develop in a post-oedipal stage. Investigating this I found, to my surprise, that Freud had for-mally named the stage after the Oedipus complex as the "father com-plex", and that the development of the superego still goes on into the latency stage from here. In contrast, Milrod's account merely emphasises internalisation of parental authority and autonomy after the Oedipus complex and ignores these subtle steps. Milrod writes:

> in the preoedipal period, fear of disapproval triggers social anxiety; fear of superego disapproval triggers superego anxiety ... which, appears with the resolution of the Oedipus complex. (p. 137) Once formed, the immediate threat of parental object loss [in the Oedipus complex] is overcome as qualities associated with the parents in the form of depersonified, abstract ideals become a part of the child's psychic structure. (p. 139) What is internalized in the crea-tion of this new structure is an array of ideal values, many coming

from the parents, along with mechanisms to enforce them. They are depersonified and abstract, carrying no personal characteristics associated with the parents. Rather than personal characteristics, it is parental authority that is internalized. Henceforth moral and ethical considerations regarding how one deals with others will be governed by the superego, which exercises its authority independent of the influence of external objects. In this way, by the time the superego is formed, the child has taken a huge step in the direction of independence from parental authority. (Milrod, 2002, p. 140)

Milrod, again and again, emphasises how external authority becomes internalised, fear of the parents becomes superego anxiety, and that the child chooses the moral values through which he also prosecutes himself. Milrod references the "depersonified" parents but doesn't reference that Freud (1926a) paired the term with social anxiety (p. 139). For Milrod, the child "exercises its authority independent of the influence of external objects" and, he even makes it sound like the child will create his own values. The parents and other "admired love objects ... *may* be the source of elements that are internalized into the superego" he writes and "society's standards, *to the degree that they are known*, will also participate" but this implies that admired love objects may not be the source and society's standards may not be known and the child creates values ex-nihilo (Milrod, 2002, p. 141, emphasis mine). I'll come back to this idea later in the section. However, before turning a critical lens on Milrod's position I'd like to give a fuller explication of Freud's. What is important for the moment is that Freud (1930, p. 125) explicitly mentions "gradual transitions" while Milrod talks of a "huge step" and Freud touts social anxiety as the form of conscience at the Oedipus complex while Milrod already sees the child choosing its own values and experiencing anxiety for not living up to its self-made assemblage of them.

As mentioned, the Oedipus complex is associated with the parental imago becoming depersonalised into the authorities, or father-substitutes, of the community. In social anxiety, the egoist fears that his immoral behaviour will be found out by them and his reputation ruined. After the Oedipus complex is overcome, then, Freud writes, the erection of religion, morality, and a "social feeling" in the following "father complex" occurs:

religion, morality, and a social sense—the chief elements in the higher side of man—were originally one and the same thing. According to the hypothesis which I put forward in Totem and Taboo they were acquired phylogenetically out of the father-complex: *religion and moral restraint through the process of mastering the* Oedipus complex *itself, and social feeling through the necessity for overcoming the* rivalry *that then remained between the members of the younger generation.* (Freud, 1923b, p. 37, emphasis mine; 1930, p. 101)

Although Freud's primal horde hypothesis is one I wouldn't defend in the form he gave it, I know that he is taking his clinical findings and trying to think historically about how they might have been generated. This historical thinking is of vital importance and psychological constants such as the Oedipus complex must be studied in both the earliest forms of culture and in their current manifestation in order to be defensible as trans-historical facts of human psychology. I'll have more to say about this soon, but for the moment I want to point out that Freud mentions the development of the superego in several different papers. He is explicit that after Oedipus it is only the nucleus of a superego that is formed:

the object-cathexes are given up and replaced by identifications. The authority of the father or the parents is introjected into the ego, and there *it forms the nucleus of the super-ego*, which takes over the severity of the father and perpetuates his prohibition against incest, and so secures the ego from the return of the libidinal object-cathexis. (Freud, 1924a, pp. 176–177, emphasis mine)

Again, we have to keep in mind that Freud, as I have shown, sometimes refers to the superego as a synonym for the guilt conscience because of its characterological importance. Here he is claiming that the Oedipus complex doesn't produce the guilt conscience but only the nucleus that will develop into the guilt conscience. Castration anxiety tied to the father's possession of the mother in the incest taboo is connected with moral fear of the father-substitutes in social anxiety. Then, after the incest taboo and castration anxiety are established, the guilt conscience arises in the father complex. Freud makes this explicit in *Inhibitions, Symptoms, and Anxiety* where he writes:

> we have already traced the change of that content from loss of
> the mother as an object to castration. The next change is caused
> by the power of the super-ego. With the depersonalisation of
> the parental agency from which castration was feared, the dan-
> ger becomes less defined. *Castration anxiety* develops into moral
> anxiety—*social anxiety*—and it is not so easy now to know what
> the anxiety is about. The formula, "separation and expulsion from
> the horde" [in the father complex], only applies to that *later por-
> tion of the super-ego* which has been formed on the basis of social
> prototypes, *not to the nucleus of the super-ego*, which corresponds
> to the introjected parental agency. (Freud, 1926a, p. 139, emphasis
> mine)

While Milrod uses "social anxiety" to denote pre-oedipal anxiety, Freud
uses the term with a specific meaning. Again, it is at the end of the
Oedipus complex when social anxiety comes into existence (Freud, 1930,
pp. 124–125). Moreover, after the instinctual renunciations that place the
individual into the father complex, in which the conscience *qua* guilt is
erected, it isn't fear of the superego at work but fear of "separation and
expulsion from the horde" that provides the fear. "The sense of guilt,"
Freud (1930) writes, "is at bottom nothing else but a topographical variety of anxiety; *in its later phases* it coincides completely with fear of the
super-ego" (p. 135, emphasis mine). He attaches signal anxiety to birth,
oral, anal, and phallic stages and explicitly writes that this fear of the
superego is in latency (Freud, 1926a, p. 142). This may sound confusing
in several ways. How can guilt be guilt if it is fear of something external? What is fear of the superego? Although the answer won't be satisfying until I anchor it deeper into phenomenology in the next section,
I can say, for the moment, that it is possible to understand fear of separation from the group as being something internal if, as I've suggested,
we come to see that dependence isn't moved from the parental imagos
to autonomy. Rather, if dependence is moved to the community—if the
"self-observation" of the superego is no longer merely for personal success but has extended to include others—then a loss of this connection
is a loss of part of oneself and therefore internal. The second question
will have to wait until I spend a little more time investigating the "early
phase" of guilt in the father complex.

If we follow Freud in recognising the development of the guilt
conscience in "phases", this naturally raises the question of what the

content of these two different forms of conscience might be. For Freud, the first post-oedipal form of the guilt conscience, which arises in the following father complex, is based upon the relationship to an imago and is compared to Kant's Categorical imperative and not any "array of ideal values". He writes:

> the super-ego retained essential features of the introjected persons— their strength, their severity, their inclination to supervise and to punish. As I have said elsewhere, it is easily conceivable that, thanks to the defusion of instinct which occurs along with this introduction into the ego, the severity was increased. The super-ego—the conscience at work in the ego—may then become harsh, cruel and inexorable against the ego which is in its charge. *Kant's Categorical Imperative is thus the direct heir of the Oedipus complex.* (Freud, 1924b, p. 167, emphasis mine; 1913, p. 22)

This conscience isn't determined by ethical traditions or by ideal values the child chooses itself, but by the "golden rule" of considering how what one does to others would feel like if done to oneself. Kant's categorical imperative is a theory that the "golden rule" is based upon judging actions by whether they would be logically possible if everyone performed the same action (Kant, 2002). The derivation of the golden rule from "pure reason" has received a lot of criticism that I don't have the space to explore now. Rather, what's important here is that some people inhibit their desires based upon some kind of respect for others. In Freud's language, the imagos of "the parents are replaced by an indefinite number of fellow-men" and one's "self-observation" becomes modified to include oneself among them—as a peer or equal (Freud, 1914b, pp. 101–102). Freud doesn't perform a metaphysical speculation about "pure reason" causing this but instead suggests a plausible psychological account of morality springing from the phantasy of one's actions being projected upon an internal image or imago. If the consequences of the same actions that now target one's self are felt as bad then the original impulses toward the object are unfair or unjust and are felt as such. The anxiety, pain, or unpleasure from this unconscious process shows up in guilt regarding one's intentions. Ultimately, anxiety at the loss of the self-observation of being a peer belonging in the community, and not merely the fear of being found out, is what establishes guilt.

The closest example that Freud offers for the mechanism of the guilt conscience is in the self-punishment meted out in a symptom. He gives the example of how the personalised aspect of the imago that is linked to the mother informs the idiosyncratic character of the symptom. Freud (1921) writes:

> let us disentangle identification as it occurs in the structure of a neurotic symptom from its rather complicated connections. Supposing that a little girl (and we will keep to her for the present) develops the same painful symptom as her mother— for instance, the same tormenting cough. This may come about in various ways. The identification may come from the Oedipus complex; in that case it signifies a hostile desire on the girl's part to take her mother's place, and the symptom expresses her object-love towards her father, and brings about a realization, under the influence of a sense of guilt, of her desire to take her mother's place: "You wanted to be your mother, and now you *are*—anyhow so far as your sufferings are concerned." This is the complete mechanism of the structure of a hysterical symptom. (Freud, 1921, p. 106)

Although Freud uses guilt to explain the blending of a personalised aspect of the imago with the self-representation, in other places he is careful to stress that "the need for punishment" shouldn't be confused with guilt because the latter's nature is to be conscious (Freud, 1924b, p. 166; 1930, p. 136). In a similar way Fairbairn (1952) has compared the internal saboteur to an "ego structure" in contrast to the superego's guilt (pp. 106–107). Additionally, Wilhelm Reich has explained the need for punishment as "the execution of a milder, substitute punishment … [and] a special kind of defense against punishment [expected from the parental substitute] and anxiety" (Reich, 1990, p. 241). Reich introduces this formulation with the masochistic character but also generally notes that when character armor, in general, is broken down "bound aggression regularly rises to the surface first" and that aggression and anxiety can be transformed into each other (ibid., p. 339). The discharge of aggression meant for parental-substitutes is the central principle for the school of "modern psychoanalysis" and improvement of schizophrenic patients has been seen through enabling them to verbalise "bottled-up anger" (Davis, 1965–1966, p. 83; Spotnitz, 1969).

In Freud's case of a hysterical symptom, a woman who is in a (defused) castration complex can triangulate with a mother-substitute and it is the aggression towards her that creates anxiety/expectation of punishment and this anxiety is defended against by punishing oneself with the symptom, as a lesser punishment. The aggression turned upon the self is then linked to the personsalised aspect of the imago (her actual mother) to form the symptom. It's not having the hysteric accept her guilty nature but rather having her express the anger she feared giving to the mother-substitute (imago) that is important.[4] There are different cases in which sin and confession of sin are important and the examination of the irrational guilt of the father complex seems needful too, but, again, my aim is to provide a framework for these conversations. What's important here is that the imago mechanism in the symptom provides an earlier form of how the guilt conscience of the father complex should be understood.

There is an important qualification to what would be a transhistorical morality. Freud seemingly contradicts the passages on the categorical imperative when he mentions that the father-complex conscience "has been formed on the basis of social prototypes" (Freud, 1926a, p. 139). Moreover, when we turn to the past and see the vast amount of sexism and racism that forbade certain individuals access to work, study, voting, etc., it's difficult to believe that the guilt conscience existed. The horrors of slavery and the systemic refutation of the abilities of women is a testament to the impunity many felt as they treated others unjustly. However, I think that what seems like a contradiction actually solves the problem of accounting for sexism and racism. If the guilt conscience values are derived from the pain or anxiety that are returned upon one by the imago, then the social input can't determine the values themselves. Therefore, I think that Freud's remark suggests that although the imago provides the values, the community/culture designates who enters into the father complex imago relation as a "person" or fellow citizen with political rights. The active-egoistic individual experiences the guilt conscience in relation to another "person", but is free to mistreat the non-person (women, slaves, etc.) so far as his passive-altruistic superego would allow it.[5]

In contrast to the father complex, the superego in its later latency form isn't based upon one's impulses to cause pain or anxiety to another being returned by the imago. Rather, the superego registers a libidinal tie to, or finds its content in, tradition. This provides the best explanation as to what Freud means when he refers to "fear of the superego" in latency in contrast to the earlier father complex guilt. In latency the "child's super-ego is in fact constructed on the model not of its parents but of its parents' super-ego" Freud writes; "the contents which fill it are the same and it becomes the vehicle of tradition and of all the time-resisting judgments of value which have propagated themselves in this manner from generation to generation" (Freud, 1933, p. 67). The latency "social ideal" represents a larger group than just "persons" or "citizens" in one's community and involves belonging to a "group mind" (Freud, 1921, p. 129). The "group minds" of race, class, creed, and nationality that Freud (1921) mentions are very much passed on to us from our parents and don't resemble an "array of values" we choose from but identities that extend past our individual narcissism that carry mores.

While oedipally the egoist is concerned with his success, love, and happiness, in the father complex his advance to morality can still see him self-absorbed in regard to his individual guilt. In latency, the "self-absorbed" child may grow to form a libidinal tie to a "self-observation" that establishes "identity" based upon the adoption of specific traditions. Some of these traditions can be sex-positive or sex-negative and therefore influence the mental health of the individual as Reich, Marcuse, and others have investigated. For example, sex-negative traditions might tout masturbation as a sin and tell the child he will suffer blindness or other types of physical degeneration and this may become a prohibition against the harmless act. However, although the narcissist hasn't developed a latency "social ideal" it shouldn't be forgotten that they want to have a good reputation and therefore can possibly back away from gratifying certain desires because of their oedipal "social anxiety". As Freud points out, they have no problem being hypocrites or leading a double life if they don't think they'll be caught.

Although Freud attempted to derive the father complex from a primal horde hypothesis that there are good reasons to doubt, one can't doubt the necessity of an imago based genesis of the guilt conscience. The values can't arise *ex-nihilo* so Freud suggests that religion, the incest-taboo/marriage, and morality all arise together when the oedipal drama, in camera obscura fashion, is projected to provide the foundation of culture. Even in Alfred Kroeber's famous essay in which Freud's primal horde hypothesis is ridiculed as a "just so" story, Kroeber writes:

however much cultural anthropology may come to lean more on the historical instead of the psychological method, it can never ultimately free itself, nor should it wish to, from the psychology that underlies it. To this psychology the psychoanalytic movement initiated by Freud has made an indubitably significant contribution, which every ethnologist must sooner or later take into consideration. (Kroeber, 1920, p. 54)

The need for psychological underpinnings to account for the rise of culture is examined in the appendix. However, in recognising that happiness is drive-based, Milrod's account isn't necessarily out of synch with this view. I mention it because it is, no doubt, a stumbling block for some other schools of psychoanalysis. But, I want to examine here is how Milrod's account of an autonomous individual assembling an array of ideal values is very much a picture of a consumer living in our age of globalisation.

Freud's model suggests that it is pre-latency drive and superego formation ("psychical constitution") that gives the child a certain character. This means that different character types exist in early cultures as they do in later ones. Some people are ambitious, some are very loyal, some are charismatic, some strive to be helpful and nice, some are impulsive, and some draw self-esteem from their beauty etc. Today's globalisation allows access to many value systems that may rationalise the individual's character. An individual who has studied a stoic or ascetic value system, for example, with the ideals of not getting attached to people or possessions, is able to offer many reasons to rationalise his pre-existing schizoid character. Ego psychologists appear to take the study of such value systems at face value without asking why a person was attracted to a system in the first place. However, an individual in a primitive political-economy does not have access to the writings and elaborated worldview of the stoics, or epicureans, or Kant's ideas of morality as duty, etc. in order to rationalise their motivations or defences. An individual there might characterologically act like a stoic, a hedonist, or someone overly conscientious about what is fair but the formalised principles that the great sages produced in different eras and different lands aren't there to legitimise the appearance of a reasoned value system.

The contemporary consumer has the freedom to make many purchases. For example, one may choose to decorate one's house in traditional Chinese style art, art from the Congo, or art from Russia. One may also choose to study the writings of Buddha, Epicetus, Kant, John Stuart Mill, to borrow the yoga sutras from the library or peruse the Old Testament in the Gideon bible of a hotel room nightstand. A globalisation that consists of both an increase of technologies of communication, as well as basic freedoms allows one to study complicated value systems, alone or with others. However, for long tracks of history religious freedom wasn't a basic freedom, any more than was the choice of one's spouse, and the many elaborated value systems weren't in wide dissemination.

The ego psychologist appears to either be over-estimating the availability of elaborated value systems in early cultures or over-estimating the average individual's interest or abilities to offer up reasoned values that direct their lives. The latter option would imply that every individual is attributed the genius of Buddha, Epicetus, Kant, Epictetus, (etc.) in thinking through, and developing reasons for, a complicated way of life. However, would an interrogation of the average person today yield an abundance of reasons for why values they profess to hold are the best ones to have? Even if someone avows allegiance to a religious value system it is doubtful that they actually studied other religions or ontological proofs for the existence of God. Although individuals today have access to many reasons for justifying their political and religious beliefs, and their feelings regarding how people should generally relate to others, many of them don't have reasoned views at all. By directing the investigation to primitive political-economies that don't have the rationalisations available, we bypass the arguments that these individuals might have less reason than average or possess multiple conflicting values. Without "an array of ideal values" the ego psychological view isn't able to provide a trans-historical model, and the pre-oedipal superego becomes much more important for future research.

V

While the Oedipus complex represents the height of the individual striving for ideals of personal happiness in success or passionate love, the subsequent father complex and latency stages concern the egoist forming "social ideals". In the ego ideal of the father complex the egoist has the "self-observation" of being "grown-up" or "adult" with the goal of being respected as such by others who are regarded as equals in the community.

The father complex is best understood as the child projecting the Oedipus complex's incest taboo on the community among his peers of the younger generation. For Freud, the end of the Oedipus complex means an internalisation of the parental imagos—of the father possessing the mother in the incest taboo—and these imagos are "depersonalised" into three important factors: First, in relation to ego drives the father imago is projected on to a "group leader" or "father-substitute" who then represents someone with authority, which is communicated through Prestige or reputation in the community. Second, in the realm of object drives the mother imago creates an "aim-inhibited" relation to "mother-substitutes" which creates an "anaclitic" love idealisation. Third, in the realm of conscience, the individual experiences "social anxiety" in regard to the community discovering that he has done something immoral.

In the following stage of the father-complex, the ego and object drives and conscience undergo a further modification. First, the individual transitions from seeking to take on the skills or knowledge from father-substitutes for egoistic self-enhancement to "social feeling" in "obeying the injunctions and prohibitions" of the "adults", "citizens", or whoever counts as a "person" in the community (Freud, 1923b, p. 37). Second, in regard to object drives, Freud's writings suggest a drive for marriage that appears to be expressed in the more humanistic formulation of genital post-ambivalent love found in Karl Abraham (1926), Wilhelm Reich (1933), and others. Third, in regards to conscience, the child recognises himself as equal to, or peer of, other "persons" in his community or group and feels guilt in regards to actions that are unjust or unfair. Finally, the latency development of the ego ideal is linked in Freud's writings to the "social ideal" and "group mind" (Freud, 1914a, 1921). In contrast to the phallic work group, which includes political parties with particular views on work life, the "group mind" of latency doesn't relate to individual narcissism. Rather it concerns social narcissism in which the individual derives pleasure from the glory or the success of the group he belongs to, without reference to his individual contribution to it.

After the resolution of the Oedipus complex the individual is still "self-absorbed". Although the active-egoist may recognise himself as less than a father-substitute, he is still taking on his education or seeking mentors for his own glory. As we saw in the last section, there is a further stage in which he must "master the Oedipus complex itself" and "overcome the rivalry ... between the member of the younger generation" in order to establish "social feeling" in the father complex (Freud, 1923b, p. 37). I've shown above that the father complex continues to be recognised in Freud's later major writings on anxiety and the superego (Freud, 1926a, 1930). However, it seems to have been conflated with the Oedipus complex by most analysts, except to the extent that they recognise the post-oedipal stage of post-ambivalent "genital" love and *social feeling*. The genital stage figures prominently in the work of Karl Abraham, Wilhelm Reich, and others, but there isn't any mention of, or tie to, the father-complex there. Moreover, using the term genital stage does not help things because it can be confused with the post-latency stage of puberty. Regardless, Karl Abraham clearly locates genitality after the Oedipus complex but still in the phallic stage and says of "social feeling" that:

> the child adopts a friendly and well-wishing attitude, first to persons of his near environment, and then to the community at large. This process seems to me to be a very important basis for the final and definitive formation of a person's character. It occurs at the time at which *the individual passes out of that phase of his libidinal development which Freud has called the phallic stage*. It implies that he has attained a point in his object-relations where he no longer has an ambivalent attitude towards the genital organ of his heterosexual object, but recognizes it as a part of that object whom he loves as an entire person ... Whereas on the earlier levels of character-development the interests of the individual and those of the community ran counter to one another, on the genital level the interests of both coincide to a great extent. (Abraham, 1926, p. 216, emphasis mine)

The idea of post-ambivalent love is expressed here in a "humanistic" formulation of loving the "entire person" that echoes the ego psychological formulation of the child having an autonomous freedom to choose its values. However, if we follow Freud's formulation, that the father complex involves mastery of the Oedipus complex between the rivals of the younger generation, then a different picture emerges. At the end of the Oedipus complex, conscience exists externally in "social anxiety" where the individual does not want the father-substitutes in the community to know the "bad" things he has done. In the father complex this becomes internalised as the guilt conscience. By analogy, post-ambivalent love in the father complex can be based upon the internalisation of the mother and father having exclusive sexual rights to each other (the incest taboo). The child then seeks not the "entire person" but instead has a drive to recreate the exclusive, monogamous relation of the parents in a desire for marriage (i.e., the active-egoist's own socially recognised, exclusive relationship to a love object).

Marriage, as I'll discuss in the conclusion, is ubiquitous in culture and for the greatest part of history has been arranged and not based upon love. Additionally, the necessity for politicians and certain public figures to be married intimates that the family unit has a libidinal value itself that others want to see. These instances illustrate how the drive to marriage is separate from love but is soldered on to it in certain cultures. Clearly, in less sophisticated political-economies with arranged marriages that secure peace from inter-group aggression, poets wouldn't be allowed to sing the praises of love and remind everyone of what they can't have or cause some to rebel against the needed institution. Moreover, practices like polyandry that exist in certain cultures show that marriage, like the guilt conscience, has room for social inputs.

In *Moses and Monotheism* Freud draws attention to this step between identification with the father and full internalisation that links the superego to pride:

> when the ego has brought the super-ego the sacrifice of an instinctual renunciation, it expects to be rewarded by receiving more love from it. The consciousness of deserving this love is felt by it as pride. At the time when the authority had not yet been internalized as a super-ego, there could be the same relation between the threat of loss of love and the claims of instinct: there was a feeling of security and satisfaction when one had achieved an instinctual renunciation out of love for one's parents. But this happy feeling could only assume the peculiar narcissistic character of pride after the authority had itself become a portion of the ego. (Freud, 1939, p. 117)

Following common language one can speak of "pride" in relation to one's children and performing one's duties, but there is another sense of pride that operates in the masculine protest/castration complex when one attempts to "be one's own father". This form of pride is captured by the pride of Lucifer leading him to rebel against God. However, understood as the recreation of the Oedipus complex among one's peers, and as a source of pride, "social feeling" in Freud's work also loses its humanistic gloss. Freud does not discuss it as a "friendly and well-wishing attitude" but instead he attempts to divine a functional approach to the imago-based relation with others. Where the father-substitutes of the Oedipus complex educate the individual into levels of symbolic Prestige and status in the community, the father-substitutes of the father complex/genital stage pass on "injunctions and prohibitions" (Freud, 1923b, p. 37). Instead of individual glory, one strives for perfection as conceived of as doing one's duty, fairness among peers, and fulfilling social obligations to others. As mentioned in the last section, the focus of the conscience is that one is a person among other persons and that equality is something to be mindful of. However, as far as the ego ideal is concerned not as a "thou shalt not" but as the "direction-giving" form of the superego, the "injunctions and prohibitions" that would comprise this drive are best described as aiming at recognition from others for one's "decency". Moreover, when one examines this attitude and combines it with the drive to marry, a general striving to be "adult" is captured. One becomes married because it is something that one ought to do. One works even if one does not like one's job because one has "responsibilities" to one's family, and one engages with others in "decent" or "polite" conversation, and talks with others in one's business about what is fair, just, and ethical because, if one does not behave in these ways then one isn't an "adult".

Although the language used to describe this may sound conscious or like the individual chooses to be adult, Freud is describing the motivational/self-esteem system that drives the individual who traverses the father complex. The drive to commitment will work in confluence with subordinate and supraordinate agencies so that the romantic love of the oedipal ego ideal and earlier drives will affect the object choice. However, if these earlier drives become defended against the individual, for example, may no longer have romantic love for his wife but still feel the need to remain in marriage to her, or enter into a passionless marriage if he is single. Similarly, an intellectual may no longer be striving to gain recognition in his field of knowledge but may turn to ethical questions and issues of fairness in dealing with other peers in the field. These individuals are driven to function this way and any consciousness of these motivations would only appear from the observation of similar behaviour in others that they apply reflexively to themselves, or what is conveyed to them from someone with this understanding. This is explored in the appendix on Wittgenstein's private language argument.

In work with "pre-genital" substance abusers, one will find active-egoistic individuals among them who don't function as adults. I've encountered several men in their forties and fifties in therapeutic group settings who have admitted that they've found women to take care of them or their children (i.e., pay for their rent and bills) and don't want to play a part in the "corrupt world". Striving for perfection *qua* "being an adult" or wanting recognition from others as a responsible "grown-up" isn't something they have ever felt as normative. Instead of thinking of these individuals as not choosing values, as Milrod would likely claim, in the Freudian model they would be seen as not having performed the instinctual renunciation to traverse the father complex and form the self-observation in which they desire to be judged as a responsible adult by others. They may have intellectual knowledge of their failure to function as "grown-ups" who have reached the father complex, and even hold regular tax-paying citizens in contempt. They feel themselves to be "exceptions" and their pride has seen them remove themselves from phallic ego drive competition with others. They function in their object drives in having a woman regard them as someone who had the potential for greatness, or who is held back from realising it, in what Kohut (1971) describes as a mirror transference. Again, this is only taking the subject egoist libidinal position into account and I'd say that many more of the group, in my experience, have been passive-altruistic.

Sticking to the structural logic of recreating the recognition of the father's moral censure, power, and possession of the mother inside oneself, social feeling likely has an aspect of competition or pride. While the child is forced to recognise its mother desires a sexual relationship with an adult in the object drives, it must also recognise its inability to acquire adult respect for its skills or knowledge in the ego drives. The child may have talents but will not have the knowledge or education required to do something to be taken seriously by adults. However, by the change of focus to fairness or morality the child now has all the intelligence to match the father. A child can surely understand, for example, that if the people who are involved are equals then fairness dictates that everyone involved in a transaction gets the same. By moving from skill to fairness the child can be an authority like the oedipal father and legitimately discuss what is fair in one's dealings with people. Although Freud (1930) into his late writings continues to mention "the part played by love [for the father] in the origin of conscience" I can't help but think there is still aggression and competition there too, and that the stage isn't the birth of autonomy but a balance of competition-aggression and restoration-affection.[6]

In parallel to the latency development of conscience, which takes its content from the specific traditions of groups within a culture, it is possible to deduce that the ego ideal would similarly take its content from the groups to which the traditions belong. As opposed to the primary narcissism of pleasure coming from phantasy or wish-making with no measurement from the ego ideal, and secondary narcissism, in which self-esteem is gained for meeting the demands for perfection of the ego ideal, a tertiary form of narcissism is suggested in Freud's writings. Perfection wouldn't be located in the individual but in the group to which the individual belongs and would thus be classified as a social narcissism. In *Group Psychology* Freud (1921) writes:

> each individual is a component part of numerous groups, he is bound by ties of identification in many directions, and he has built up his ego ideal upon the most various models. Each individual therefore has a share in numerous group minds—those of his race, of his class, of his creed, of his nationality, etc. (Freud, 1921, p. 129)

Later in *Future of an Illusion* he writes:

> the satisfaction which the ideal offers to the participants in the culture is thus of a narcissistic nature; it rests on their pride in what has already been successfully achieved … On the strength of these differences every culture claims the right to look down on the rest … The narcissistic satisfaction provided by the cultural ideal … can be shared in not only by the favored classes, which enjoy the benefits of the culture, but also by the suppressed ones, since the right to despise the people outside it compensates them for the wrongs they suffer within their own unit. No doubt one is a wretched plebian, harassed by debts and military service; but, to make up for it, one is a Roman citizen, one has one's share in the task of ruling other nations and dictating their laws. (Freud, 1927a, p. 13)

One can be a poor American harassed by collection agencies and social services, but one is American! And, even though one does not have a passport and has never travelled anywhere else, one can know that America is the best place in the world. This new social ideal in one's class, race, or nation becomes something one strives to give glory to and from which one receives pride. Even though I recognised the "social input" of class in the father complex as determining who is a "person", the latency version goes beyond the adult acceptance of the "way of the world" and the limitations of birth or caste. In *Denial of Death* Ernest Becker (1973) contrasts the individual striving for immortality to species or group immortality in serving one's country, one's religion, class, or race and passing these values on to one's children. Imperatives to "buy American" and do what's good for the American economy as opposed to what's good for oneself or one's family are normative. Moreover, the "American character" as an identity becomes normative and being "freedom-loving", "a maverick", or other such stereotypes become part of one's identity. Additionally, it is clear that such group minds exist on a smaller level. For example, there are municipal group minds illustrated in the social narcissist's pleasure in the success of their local teams, despite having played no role in this success. Their moods are nevertheless thoroughly affected by the team's performance and this illustrates the part it plays in their self-esteem system.

It is also possible to witness political rhetoric that does not seek to reach people in regard to their individual narcissism (their own personal success, power, or duty) but which appeals to them, as Freud mentions, as a class. The appeal to their group narcissism is often paired with an appeal to earlier defused ego ideal fears. For example, the rhetoric around "Obamacare" was about the "nanny state", which was portrayed as wanting to make decisions for the individual, control him, become bigger and bigger and overwhelm him, and take away his freedom, on one hand. On the other hand, there was an appeal to class traditions, and certain ideologues would say things like, "Some people don't want to be sipping chardonnay from a crystal stem, they want to be drinking beer from a red Solo Cup. You know? Choices" (Blackburn, 2013). Class pride in one's lower class, beer-drinking traditions is exalted above the pretentious tastes of the upper classes. Politicians pander to this pride to obscure the rational investigation of the outcome of the affordable healthcare act that may benefit one individually. This latency development deserves much more examination, but this is the point in which interdisciplinary work must begin. My interest here is only to point to this sphere of social narcissism in order to grant relief to the father complex and indicate how Freud suggests the superego develops post-oedipally.

In summary, the egoist who doesn't perform the instinctual renunciation to enter the father complex/genital phase can be broadly characterised as narcissistic in the sense that he is self-absorbed and only has a "self-observation" for his own personal success. This leaves the individual open to narcissistic injuries (ego drives) and betrayals in sexual relationships (object drives) that can result in neurotic introversion of the libido to earlier stages that result in the person becoming less able to engage in work or love. As mentioned above, Freud and Adler observed this in criminality and abusive relationships.

The individual who has formed "genital" character through traversing the father complex has formed a post-ambivalent tie to others that anchors him against the regression of the libido from the Oedipus complex. His ideal to be regarded by others as an adult means that he may retain some object constancy in his relationships and offset the sado-masochistic impulses that appear with defusion from the Oedipus complex. Additionally, he may stay in a job that he doesn't like or find satisfying for the sake of his family and to do his duty. However, the individual who has attained genital character may still be "self-absorbed" in his irrational feelings of guilt even though he has more constancy in his relations (Freud, 1931b).[7]

If an individual develops to the latency ego ideal then he goes beyond the potential self-absorption to social narcissism. To be clear, an individual might not traverse the father complex nor form a guilt conscience but still develop psychosexually to form a latency social ideal. When oedipal regression occurs in those with latency ideals they may retain ties to the world with the anchor of linguistically mediated identities through the libidinal ties to various group minds, but, following the writings of Nietzsche (1886), Ortega y Gasset (1930), and others it registers as conformity with the passions of the drives lost. Such authors criticise the "mass man" or "herd" for the absence of drives to perfection and passionate love and the mediocrity they are satisfied with. If I am correct, Freud's model does speak to their concerns while offering a sobering view of the self-absorption involved with the narcissist and his preoccupation with perfection.

Lastly, two other points seem salient in the economics of libido. The narcissistic structure, having fewer ties that his psychic energy must sustain, may be capable of greater achievements if he avoids defusion and regression. Additionally, it is also important to recognise that having romantic relationships (object drives) allows the individual to buffer some of the potential narcissistic injuries he might receive in his public life (ego drives). Sex-negative cultures that make pre-marital romance difficult to indulge in without shame, or supply a potential latency superego tradition or mos that becomes part of the latency guilt conscience, will leave the economy of libido more likely to sustain a narcissistic injury by putting all the emphasis on the ego drives. Culture is so variable that the reverse of this—putting too much emphasis on the object drives and having sanctions against displays of individual competition and glory—is, no doubt, also to be found.

Conclusion

I have contrasted two basic pictures of the human being in this chapter. One picture is that of the primarily separate or atomistic, rational chooser. He is defined by possessing a "will" and by "deciding", for example, to be ambitious or not and deciding to do something wrong instead of something right. The other picture is that of the primarily related, conflict-based view of the individual. He is defined not by choosing but by being driven to relate to others in certain ways. I have argued that ego psychologists such as Milrod attempt to refine the first model by acknowledging that the individual is initially related and driven to strive for happiness, but then they seek to recreate the rational chooser model when it comes to the guilt conscience. I've argued that Freud's view of morality is imago-based and doesn't involve an autonomous value choosing. I've also argued that Freud's view is more feasible because it provides a trans-historical model while the autonomy model of ego psychology can't claim that the elaborate ideal values found in globalisation are available to determine behaviour in every historical period.

I've recognised the input of ideal values in three ways. The first concerns the ability of an individual to make and hold himself to promises, but the content of such promises need not have moral content. An individual can swear a vendetta, for example, just as he can take an oath that might have something resembling moral content. However, it arises in the context of his relationships and group dynamics—not from the ethical needs of the birth of some kind of autonomy. The second form of ideal values concerns how they enter as different practical relations to fairness and the feeling of equality with others in the community in what Freud (1923b, p. 37) terms "social feeling". An individual belongs to various work groups, leagues, and social clubs and must mediate his practices there with his equality with others and the inequality brought about by different classes. Freud associates the third form with the development of latency. At this time the individual leaves the self-absorbed striving for his own happiness, whether active-egoistic or passive-altruistic, and forms an identity based upon participation in different *group minds* (Freud, 1921, p. 129). One forms a self-observation based upon race, class, creed, and nationality that affect one's desires and internalises traditions. Although, the pre-genital narcissist wants an image of goodness, fairness, and obedience to important mores, the values concern his reputation and are not linked to his "self-observation" of being equal to others.

I've followed some of Freud's suggestive comments and created a structural relation between the Oedipus complex and the following father complex. As the moral father the father imago at the Oedipus complex can judge one's moral failings and this creates "social anxiety". As the more knowledgeable, skilled, or wise father he represents a leader who the subject egoist can receive education from. As the father who possesses the mother's love in the "incest taboo" he provides a template for the union of man and woman and the subject egoist idealises someone of the opposite sex in his or her generation in the object drive relation. These forms of the parental imagos appear to become mastered by the subject egoist establishing his relations between his siblings or peers. He erects a guilt conscience in which fear for the loss of reputation or authorities finding out is replaced by guilt for a bad intention or transgression because he observes himself as a peer of other persons or citizens in the community. Just as the father imago is a relationship of transference to those with more skill or knowledge, the subject egoist seeks to be someone who is an authority in setting the standards of politeness and fairness ("prohibitions and injunctions") with peers in social feeling. In regard to the object drives the permanence of the mother and father's union in the incest taboo is mastered as seeking commitment and the family for oneself.

If we take the oedipal mother and father imagos as providing the template for the superego at the father complex/genital stage, then not only do we make sense of Freud's writings, but we are able to make important connections to psychopathology, group psychology, anthropology, and sociology. If, following ego psychology, we make Oedipus into everything then we lose the ability to make nuanced applications of psychoanalytic theory.

In the oedipal incest taboo the mother and father are seen as above oneself, or as a different generation, then the logical implication is that the following stage of the father complex would have to come from an id object choice that is non-parental. If the boy selects the mother again as a sex object then the incest-taboo/difference between the generations wouldn't really have been internalised. This has two important corollaries. First, where love for a brother or sister is often taken to be "displaced" love for parents, it might actually be the case that sibling love has its own direct impulse. Additionally, before heterosexual marriage (recreation of the father and mother's exclusive relationship) becomes a drive, Freud and others suggest the renunciation of homosexual desires in the boy for those of the younger generation. Freud writes:

> the ego ideal ... has a social side; it is also the common ideal of a family, a class or a nation. It binds not only a person's narcissistic libido, but also a considerable amount of his homosexual libido, which is in this way turned back into the ego. The want of satisfaction which arises from the non-fulfilment of this ideal liberates homosexual libido, and this is transformed into a sense of guilt (social anxiety). Originally this sense of guilt was a fear of punishment by the parents, or, more correctly, the fear of losing their love; later the parents are replaced by an indefinite number of fellow-men. (Freud, 1914b, pp. 101–102)

Although Freud originally included the family with class and nation, we've seen he later defines the group mind of latency as including a libidinal tie to the groups of race, class, creed, nationality, etc. (Freud, 1921, p. 129). Additionally, he also refines his use of guilt to denote only the post-oedipal conscience that includes feeling badly about intentions and anxiety that concerns the self-observation of being a peer among other citizens in the community. The homosexual libido he observes is often attributed to the passive-altruistic pole of the personality but several writers have indicated that such impulses can also be found in the active-egoistic pole. McDougal (1989a) writes:

> certain fundamental factors that contribute to sexual identity formation and its inversions, in particular the importance of the different identifications with both parents that essentially structure the sense of sexual identity for all children. Here several psychic dramas intertwine: the one to receive most attention in our psycho-analytic literature is the heterosexual oedipal crisis which involves, among other important factors, the wish to possess in the most literal sense of the word the parent of the opposite sex while wishing death upon the same-sex parent. But there is also the homosexual oedipal drama which also implies a double aim, that of having exclusive possession of the same-sex parent and that of being the parent of the opposite sex. (McDougall, 1989a, p. 206)

If homosexual impulses on the active-egoistic pole exist at the Oedipus complex then they must also respect the difference between the generations and find a new aim in siblings or those of the younger generation after the incest taboo. In the Book *Phallos: A Symbol and Its History in the Male World,* author Thorkil Vanggaard (1972) details the "homosexual radical" that exists in men and has existed in various cultural practices of pederasty that pass on manhood to boys. These practices usually lasted until puberty and Vanggaard differentiates this homosexual impulse from the feminine part of the personality. There are also other analysts who continued to affirm Freud's homosexual impulses and their relation to the ego ideal and note the involvement of a brother in their aim (Hymer, 1984; K. Lewes, 1998).

The second corollary is that if the child has the intention of respecting the differences between the generations then Freud's initial seduction theory is important for some cases of pathology. Specifically, classic theorists like Wilhelm Reich cite hysteria as having a fixation at the genital stage with the father (Reich, 1933, p. 177, 206). The work of a more recent psychotherapist has stressed that one out of every forty-three women is a victim of incest with the biological father and that this is seven times more likely with a step-father (Johnson, 1994, p. 241). This isn't even counting sexualised play, looking/inneundo, and other veiled forms. This work seems to suggest the importance of this exploitation of the girl's sexuality by someone of the elder generation. Additionally, the sexual link between an external moral authority and a child is seen in the many priests charged with molesting children. This difference between the generations and an external rather than internal moral authority in this case suggests a similar post-oedipal seduction of the boy by the father or a male of the elder generation. The priest might be re-enacting the sexuality of his father who, transgressing the difference between the generations, molested or sexually over-stimulated the priest as a child.

In the realm of anthropology, Levi-Strauss has gone far to show the universality of incest taboos among siblings and cousins within culture. It was in seeing this cultural incest taboo that I had the idea that the child might be recreating the oedipal incest taboo and this made my eye sensitive to mastery in other forms. In an important feminist essay, anthropologist Gayle Rubin notes that "the precision of fit between Freud and Levi-Strauss is striking. Kinship systems require a division of the sexes. The oedipal phase divides the sexes" (Rubin, 1975, p. 198). However, Rubin ends up taking a Lacanian version of the Oedipus complex and sees the division of the sexes as cultural, leading to compulsory heterosexuality, and something contingent that could, and should, be restructured. By doing so she ignores the notion of post-ambivalent love that is attached to the genital stage and marriage and the difference between the Oedipus and father complex/genital stage in general. However, her work does draws attention to how the recreation of the mother and father's exclusive relationship (in the incest taboo) in the drive for marriage could also mean that gender divisions become important in the ego drives of the father complex. Rubin shows that men and women, through cultural institutions, have to do different labour and that this amounts to something of a taboo against "social hermaphroditism" which "exacerbates the biological differences between the sexes and thereby creates gender" (ibid., p. 178). This means that the formalised, "decent", or "adult" gender relations of the father complex have to be contrasted to the "difference between the sexes" that is established in the ego ideal after the Oedipus complex. Rubin's work also shows that there are social inputs into the ideal of marriage that fits with the parallel of social inputs into the guilt conscience.

Freud's formulation of the father complex also has very important ties to group psychology. Freud (1921) famously examined the way that a mob could act in such a way as to overpower the individual's conscience. However, this form of group psychology must be earlier than the phallic-oedipal if the latter relates to a leader concerned with education and work life and the father complex concerns fairness or justice concerning "persons" in one's culture. As mentioned above, Freud saw the ego ideal at work in other mammals such as wolves and this suggests both that more primitive forms of the ego ideal exist and that the primal horde hypothesis might be indicating an earlier Oedipus complex or triangulation. Additionally, this keeps with the observation that aggression in development is first manifested as physical destruction against the bodies of others and only later becomes refined to actual sadism in which the aim is the enjoyment of the pain or humiliation caused to the other person. If this division holds up then a triangle that involves killing one's rival should signify an earlier Oedipus complex and that the phallic-oedipal concerns aggression towards the rival's image or reputation. This follows Klein's findings, in her early writing, that caused her to initially move the Oedipus complex back to two years (Klein, 1927). It also captures Kohut's observation that "competition with superior rivals which are followed by experiences of retribution fears ... [leave] no doubt about the fact that the activated conflicts belong to the castration complex of the phallic-oedipal phase" (Kohut, 1971, p. 154). This conflation between the two levels makes sense if one understands that so long as defusion exists on both the phallic and the earlier stage, then both the social and the physical anxieties would manifest together (ibid., p. 153).

Freud's closest formulation of the group psychology of the father complex conscience comes from its relation to justice:

> social justice means that we deny ourselves many things so that others may have to do without them as well, or, what is the same thing, may not be able to ask for them. This demand for equality is the root of social conscience and the sense of duty. It reveals itself unexpectedly in the syphilitic's dread of infecting other people, which psycho-analysis has taught us to understand. The dread exhibited by these poor wretches corresponds to their violent struggles against the unconscious wish to spread their infection on to other people; for why should they alone be infected and cut off from so much? ... Thus social feeling is based upon the reversal of what was first a hostile feeling into a positively toned tie in the nature of an identification ...—its demand that equalization shall be consistently carried through. (Freud, 1921, p. 121)

Freud's use of the demand for equality between persons and its relation to social feeling suggests that political beliefs or attitudes are also part of drive and superego-based character. We might imagine a contemporary example of the underlying phantasy as: "If I got laid off and I couldn't find a job immediately, I would like social assistance until I was on my feet. Therefore I can't refuse this to others". For Freud, group psychology functions by an internalised conscience being regressively placed upon an external father-substitute who becomes the arbiter of right and wrong. As we've seen, this follows the structure of the imago developmentally. If we take the example of externalising one's conscience against physically destructive acts upon a mob leader that leads to lynching, looting, or harming others, then Freud's remark that "we deny ourselves many things so that others may have to do without them as well" is an example of group psychology at the level of the political. The conscience of the father complex would be externalised onto an ideologue, "opinion leader", or party spokesman who represents the oedipal father-substitute that the individual fears in social anxiety. By identifying with the father-substitutes who have Prestige and externalising one's superego onto them, the subject-egoist gets to sadistically enjoy the thought of those denied social assistance suffering or experiencing shame even though it might be in the egoist's own interest to have such a measure in place.

Lastly, there is a major omission of religion and the concept of God in my investigation. Freud holds that along with morality and marriage that religion is institutionalised in the father complex. I would have liked to have examined the concept of God here but the influence of more archaic and powerful parental images of the pre-oedipal period would surely play a part as much as the phallic-oedipal and father-complex contributions. Working with schizophrenics it is apparent that they have a concept of God that is important in their delusions. In parallel to phantasies of different types of impregnation (oral, anal, etc.) their delusions involving God and the devil are very idiosyncratic and don't seem to be based upon the religious traditions of the community. Additionally, the failure of the schizophrenic to surmount the father complex and have an anchor in marriage, family, and duty when oedipal defusion occurs suggests that the libidinal tie to God must happen at the Oedipus complex. This has some support in the shared language of one's father and God both being procreators—one of the individual and one of the world.

A greater investigation of the concept of God and its involvement in pathology and group psychology must be carried out, but I would like to recognise the importance the institution of the church or fellowship of believers plays in sociology. When we consider religion as a social institution, it obviously has an important role in explaining who does and who doesn't count as a person in God's view. Here it isn't psychoanalysis but Marxian sociology that will have explanatory power. Religious institutions can't be considered in isolation from class and since the bible has been used to defend slavery/abolish slavery, suppress women/liberate women, etc., the phantasies found within it can't be seen as causal in regard to forming the views of those who possess the church, along with the family, as a social ideal. Rather, the interests of the wealthy or ruling classes—meaning the study of Marxian sociology—is more important for understanding religion *qua* institution. However, when specific myths and rites of religion are examined mere economics and class can't explain the symbols and irrational desires involved. Psychoanalysis can show how particular myths and rites of religion issue from psychosexual developmental points. Ultimately, until both psychoanalyst and Marxist realise that they have been telling a one-sided story that has resulted in both being excommunicated from the university system then both will rightly continue to exist as outcasts.

By returning to Freud's model of a primarily related individual who is driven to find happiness, and avoiding the neat resolution offered by ego psychologists, psychoanalytic concepts gain a lot of traction in other disciplines. However, Freud's Copernican revolution is, as he foresaw, a giant blow to the ego of those who need to feel that they choose their own happiness or, at least, choose to be good. If I am correct, psychoanalysis may have made several advancements since Freud but, in very important ways, it has lost the complexity and the scope he initially laid out. I hope to have adequately directed my reader to appreciate his work and to have pointed to inspiring connections for those who hunger for more rigour in psychoanalytic theory and have the courage to face the political implications of recognising our primary relatedness and dependence.

Notes

1. Fairbairn writes "that intellectual pursuits as such, whether literary, artistic, scientific, or otherwise, appear to exercise a special attraction for individuals possessing schizoid characteristics to one degree or another. Where scientific pursuits are concerned, the attraction would

appear to depend upon the schizoid individual's attitude of detachment no less than upon his overvaluation of the thought-processes; for these are both characteristics which readily lend themselves to capitalization within the field of science. The obsessional appeal of science, based as this is upon the presence of a compulsive need for orderly arrangement and meticulous accuracy, has, of course, long been recognized; but the schizoid appeal is no less definite and demands at least equal recognition. Finally the statement may be hazarded that a number of outstanding historical figures lend themselves to the interpretation that they were either schizoid personalities or schizoid characters; and indeed it would appear as if it were often such who leave a mark upon the page of history" (Fairbairn, 1952, p. 6).

2. Freud (1917a) was open to the idea of the ego relation to parents being parallel to the sexual relation and even taking the lead: "it is not our belief that a person's libidinal interests are from the first in opposition to his self-preservative interests; on the contrary, the ego endeavours at every stage to remain in harmony with its sexual organization as it is at the time and to fit itself into it. The succession of the different phases of libidinal development probably follows a prescribed programme. But the possibility cannot be rejected that this course of events can be influenced by the ego, and we may expect equally to find a certain parallelism, a certain correspondence, between the developmental phases of the ego and the libido; indeed a disturbance of that correspondence might provide a pathogenic factor" (Freud, 1917a, pp. 351–352). My reference to the psycho-social is to the social dimension of the ego drives in relation to the "depersonalised" father imago I just discussed.

3. This doesn't mean that one can't consciously avow one's motivation for doing something. One can, for example, say "I did x to get revenge" and be correct in the sense that revenge was the strongest motivation but there might be other drives that express themselves in that act. However, to say that one decided to not get revenge as if one simply chose not to do so doesn't take into account the potential fear of getting caught, the fear of retribution, the perception of the satisfaction it might give the other to see you reduced to this, the guilt one might feel, and any other potential motivation. By positing drives Freud simply claims that every act has a motivation and that actions are often over-determined and have several drives/motivations that they satisfy. Logic or reason is a secondary phenomenon that is in the service of a particular desire, drive, or feeling.

4. Personally I can attest to the improvement of many object egoists who have been able to express their impulses to "strangle" their mother-substitutes. In a psychotic case the patient often explicitly

referred to the feeling of being strangled herself before she recounted a story of triangulation in which she could voice the desire to strangle the other woman.

5. If one looks to history he or she will see that our current time's inclusiveness in political rights and access to public institutions for women and different races is unprecedented. Although culture does not progress in a straight line of development and there are moments when barbarism returns, civilisation can be viewed as a gradual development of inclusion for groups that had been previously marginalised or discounted: slaves, those of other cultures, women, (etc.). Civilisation, in this sense, is also the slow removal of socially sanctioned targets of aggression as they come to be included in the father complex guilt conscience. Again, I'd like to stress, that this is only from the viewpoint of the active-egoistic pole of the personality and that ethical life would also be informed by the passive-altruistic pole of the personality.

If this is the nature of the guilt conscience then the work of Freud could dovetail nicely with a teleological view of history. This teleological view of history has its roots in the philosophy of Hegel and continues with sociologists like Norbert Elias—although the latter wouldn't characterise his work this way (Elias, 1994, p. xi). Hegel's concept of who is seen as free views the teleology from the stance of political power while Elias views the teleology from the stance of the individual making a renunciation of the expression of aggression. While the former view requires a psychological motivation for regarding others as equal, the latter requires the renunciation of aggression to be tied to a new perceived equality or peerage with others. This may not be as a full peer but as at least a person who has dignity and deserves some respect.

Hegel writes: "[w]orld history is the record of the spirit's efforts to attain knowledge of what it is in itself. The Orientals do not know that the spirit or man as such are free in themselves. And because they do not know that, they are not themselves free. They only know that One is free …. The consciousness of freedom first awoke among the Greeks, and they were accordingly free; but, like the Romans, they only knew that Some, and not all men as such, are free …. The Germanic nations, with the rise of Christianity, were the first to realize that All men are by nature free, and that freedom of spirit is his very essence" (Hegel, 1975, p. 54).

Elias (1994) writes: "[i]f members of present-day western civilized society were to find themselves suddenly transported into a past epoch of their own society, such as the medieval-feudal period, they would find there much they esteem 'uncivilized' in other societies today. Their reaction would scarcely differ from that produced in them at present by the behaviour of people in feudal societies outside the Western World (p. ix) …. The distance in their behaviour and whole psychical structure between children and adults increases in the course of the civilizing process. Here, for example, lies the key to the question of why some peoples or groups of peoples appear to us as 'younger' or 'more childlike', others as 'older' or 'more grown-up'. What we are trying to express in this way are differences in the kind and the stage of a civilizing process that these societies have attained …. Nothing would be more absurd than to look for an 'agrarian feudal age' or a 'Renaissance' or a 'courtly-absolutist period' in the life of individuals. All concepts of this kind refer to the structure of whole social groups … [children] must indeed pass through a civilizing process in order to reach the standard attained by their society in the course of its history, but not through the individual phases of the social civilizing process" (p. xi).

6. To put this in to context, in the next chapter, I argue that subject altruist at the father complex would have competition finally balance with his or her affection. This is in contrast to the subject egoist who defuses in the castration complex to become self-absorbed and care only for his or her own success or power. The subject altruist who defuses returns to drives that place others first and becomes self-effacing or self-sacrificing of her desires for the desires of others. Guilt in the father complex is about being unfair to others in the egoist and "owing it to oneself" to have independence and be assertive in the altruist.

7. "The second type is what I have termed the *obsessional* type—a name which may at first seem strange. It is distinguished by the predominance of the super-ego, which is separated from the ego under great tension. People of this type are dominated by fear of their conscience instead of fear of losing love. They exhibit, as it were, an internal instead of an external dependence. They develop a high degree of self-reliance; and, from the social standpoint, they are the true, pre-eminently conservative vehicles of civilization" (Freud, 1931b, p. 218).

CHAPTER THREE

"We cannot fall out of this world": psychoanalysis and social ontology

The Cartesian or popular Western view of the mind claims that the mind is whole or "indivisible" and in its essence, logical. A person chooses or "wills" to study or work hard and if she is poor or ignorant she is responsible for it. However, this view cannot account for the breaks of the mind in mental illness except to say that something has gone wrong with the body—the passions cloud one's mind or a chemical imbalance interferes with reason issuing its commands. Moreover, this view of the mind as a conflict free zone in which "the self" or ego is in control is not rooted in any empiricism. As Nietzsche (2000) points out, it's not as if one gets to choose what ideas come to mind. An idea comes to mind when *it* wants, and so one can't claim to have determined the stream of consciousness. Because we don't have the phenomenal experience of choosing what ideas come to mind this leads many people to Kant's famous antimonies and the declaration that it is impossible to know whether an internal rational self causes the ideas or whether there are multiple drives and ideals that cause them. The philosopher Wittgenstein argues that we can follow the *use* of language in important ways to get past this antimony and I'd like to direct the reader to the appendix for these arguments. However, my interest here isn't in philosophical arguments but in psychology.

I want to examine Freud's observation that the existence of mental illness should provide us with some understanding of how the mind is put together:

> if we throw a crystal to the floor, it breaks; but not into haphazard pieces. It comes apart along its lines of cleavage into fragments whose boundaries, though they were invisible, were predetermined by the crystal's structure. Mental patients are split and broken structures of this same kind. Even we cannot withhold from them something of the reverential awe which peoples of the past felt for the insane. They have turned away from external reality, but for that very reason they know more about internal, psychical reality and can reveal a number of things to us that would otherwise be inaccessible to us. (Freud, 1917b, p. 58)

In order to account for mental illness, Freud performs a Copernican revolution in relation to the rational will. He doesn't offer philosophical arguments but claims that there is empirical data to be accounted for, and if we simply claim that the mind is rational and indivisible we can't account for the breaks in it. Thus, in Freud's model humans are "driven" to relate to others in the form of different motivational structures that give us a primarily social nature. By considering the individual to be comprised of different egoistic and altruistic motivations, and the failure to compete with or restore others as defensive or pathological, Freud accounts for the breaks of the mind, as Copernicus accounts for the motion of the planets: by de-centring the investigation. In this model "the will" is "directed by ... reports" from:

> a hierarchy of superordinated and subordinated agencies, a labyrinth of impulses striving independently of one another towards action, corresponding with the multiplicity of instincts and of relations with the external world, many of which are antagonistic to one another and incompatible. (Freud, 1917a, p. 141)

Freud doesn't write about a single superordinate agency internalised after the Oedipus complex here but instead posits "a hierarchy of superordinated and subordinated agencies". In other places Freud refers to the superordinated agencies through their internalisation as imagos that form the superego throughout development. He writes:

nor must it be forgotten that a child has a different estimate of its parents at different periods of its life. At the time at which the Oedipus complex gives place to the super-ego they are something quite magnificent; but later they lose much of this. Identifications then come about with these later parents as well, and indeed they regularly make important contributions to the formation of character; *but in that case they only* affect *the ego, they no longer influence the* super-ego, *which has been determined by the earliest parental imagos.* (Freud, 1933, p. 64, emphasis mine; 1923b, p. 48)

In the classical psychoanalytic model the child attributes different forms of perfection to the parents and through primary identification with, or permanent introjection of, these estimates, she forms an imago of this sense of power. From this imago she is both compelled to be perfect herself (active form) or devote herself to the perfection of a parental substitute (passive form). The subject of this chapter is how we are to understand these various forms of perfection and their relations to the breakdown of the mind. Although others have drawn attention to Freud's Copernican revolution before, and its de-centring, most notably Laplanche (1999), this relation hasn't been adequately examined. Rather, Freud is treated like a child who got as much wrong as he got right, and who, in the end, didn't really understand what his contribution was.

In this chapter I argue that Freud conceives of perfection as a negative quality. Perfection isn't an idea that a finite mind can grasp, instead, the perfection aimed is descriptive of relationships. It comes from understanding that humans are social animals. The different forms are small independent systems that comprise different states of "being" or what comprises the subject of ontology in philosophy. In Freud's Copernican revolution, in which the mind is built up from the *instinctual renunciations* and *primary identifications* with the caregivers to form the subordinate and superordinate agencies—in which humans are understood as primarily related—it is more precise to call it social ontology.

In the first chapter I argued that Freud's active *vs.* passive distinction is more clearly represented as the conflict between egoism and altruism and that many major analysts have corroborated this in their own jargon-based form. Although I further complemented the two subject positions of egoism and altruism by two different object positions, I would like to stick with the two, more straightforward, subject positions to further argue that to negate the finite not only leads to perfection but also to death and that the latter is the deep structure of altruism. The treatment of all the libidinal positions and their nuclear complexes will be an undertaking that requires many clinical and cultural examples and my hope is just to sketch the outline for this project so others may join me.

I

In the last chapter I indicated that Freud sees that the inter-relation of the ego and object drives and the imagos of the superego is based upon the genesis of each. In the first movement an "id object choice" or "erotic object choice" is formed for the mother or mother's body that must be "instinctually renounced" to form the ego and object drives (Freud, 1920, p. 42; 1923b, pp. 29–30). Although Freud compares active-egoistic ego drives to Adler's will to power, mastery, "magnification of the individual", and often returns to the bland designation of self-preservation, his most interesting and important formulation is the one involving "perfection" (1917a, p. 137; 1924b, p. 163; Freud, 1933, p. 96). I will return to it shortly. Following the creation of the ego and object drives comes the primary identification or permanent introjection that enshrines the estimate of the father's perfection in the imago (Freud, 1917b, p. 329; 1921, p. 105; 1923b, pp. 28–34; 1914b, p. 94). Freud's use of the perfection of the imago overlaps with his use of the perfection aimed at in the ego drive. Freud was aware of this and lamented that "so long as the ego works in full harmony with the super-ego it is not easy to distinguish between their manifestations; but tensions and estrangements between them make themselves very plainly visible" (Freud, 1938, p. 206). However, although Freud lost his confidence to differentiate between the two I think the formulation is there in his earlier work.

In *Beyond the Pleasure Principle* Freud (1920) writes that the "drive for perfection" isn't based upon some innate idea of perfection but instead it is based upon the id impulse being blocked from fulfillment. I take this to mean it becomes a negative quality that "never ceases to strive for complete satisfaction" because "there is … no prospect of bringing the process to a conclusion or of being able to reach the goal" (ibid., p. 42). Freud's claim here is a simple one. The finite mind couldn't possibly grasp something infinite or perfect even though some philosophers have claimed the opposite. Freud "naturalistically" proposes that concepts like perfection can't have their existence in the individual's grasp of innate ideas. Rather, they can be conceptualised negatively in the primary relatedness of individuals. This is not as some kind of negative thought in an atomistic individual but the assumption that transference in its most general form is always there as a felt reaction that is coupled with different types of anxiety. Later, words, as tools, can be used to describe functional modes of behaviour that reflect the different types of transference and an individual can consciously avow these motivating drives for perfection. For example, when an individual says I want to be "the top of the class", "the best guitarist people have ever seen", or "I don't want him to desire anyone but me" it can register the sense of perfection involved. Again, the motivations exist in our social nature.

In the last chapter I explicated the centrality of the Oedipus complex issues from its place as the apex of passionate love relations (object drives), as well as from the striving for happiness that is located in success (ego drives) in the subject egoistic. Both of these drives are modified by the ego ideal that possesses a "double kind of tie" that allows the individual to put another person in his ego ideal (Freud, 1921, p. 130). I showed that in other texts Freud links this same capacity to the imago, which, as we've seen, he holds to "determine" the superego. For example, in the "Economic problem of masochism" Freud writes that "the Oedipus complex … [the parent's] personal significance for the superego recedes into the background" and "the imagos they leave behind … link [to] the influences of teachers and authorities …" (Freud, 1924b, pp. 167–168). Chasseguet-Smirgel's formulation that the Oedipus complex has a maturational quality that acknowledges "the difference between the generations" also captures this formulation very nicely (Chasseguet-Smirgel, 1976b, p. 354, 358; 1976a, p. 282).

I also outlined that the "double tie" in which one can put a father-substitute in one's ego drive ego ideal as the quintessential example of eros or fusion of the drives. While in fusion with the father imago the egoistic is able to have friendly relations with others who are also under the father, and can put the work first and recognise the talents of others (Freud, 1921, p. 130). The egoistic under eros will have regulated self-esteem with the trust that he'll take on the father's knowledge and be where he is someday. The Oedipus complex proper is whatever causes the individual to defuse from the father imago and taking a father-substitute. The first stage of defusion, which I align with phobos, indicates the fear of taking a father-substitute in what is classically termed the castration complex. The egoistic is no longer willing to be under the father-substitute and, essentially, strives to possess the phallus himself or become his own father in what Freud recognises as the social manifestation of the castration complex by citing Alfred Adler's "masculine protest" (Freud, 1914b; Freud, 1937). In the castration complex self-esteem is no longer regulated because the ego ideal is an individual ego ideal and is suffused with feelings of inferiority. Although a sense of "narcissistic triumph" may occasionally be felt in defusion—when the ego coincides with the ego ideal—"it is from its nature only possible as an episodic phenomenon" (Freud, 1930, p. 76). The individual feels that he is as powerful as his father imago for a spell, but the negative quality of the drive means that it quickly goes away.

The fusion with father imago is the recognition of the Prestige of the father-substitute for holding a position or having accreditation from the social order. In defusion the individual experiences the "thou shalt" tension of becoming his own father (Freud, 1923b, pp. 54–55). Regarding a field of knowledge we can see these differences registered in the attainment of GSCE's and A Levels (high school diploma), BA, MA, doctorate, (etc.) and continue for those who have a better job at a more recognised institution or more publications. Outside of knowledge there are different levels of sports leagues and different rankings between the teams. In the world of business one's skill is measured in the money one earns and membership to certain clubs. Those who earn significantly more or are part of prestigious organisations will receive the phallic father transference. However, Prestige isn't just someone's status in the community but also can be based upon an individual competing with another and seeing his superiority in comparison. What is important here is that it's possible to see that those in higher positions of authority aren't always more skilled or knowledgeable, so that transference is seen not to be mediated purely through language. In defusion, the individual appears to have chosen to take back some transference, which we could identify as respect, from those with Prestige in the community or authority in the workplace. As Reich (1990) notes, we see in these cases the inability to take "subordinate positions in the rank and file" and criticisms regarding the work group leaders (Reich, 1990, pp. 123, 217–218).

The Janus-faced quality of the phallic father transference in regards to status/authority and ability means that the phallic drive, or striving for perfection at the phallic level, is best understood in regard to an *image-ego*. The individual wants to be admired for doing *some*thing. The image-ego is easily observable in the child's desire for mastery of specific skills (i.e., somersaults, swinging a baseball bat, recounting certain memorised facts) or interest in certain subjects. He wants the admiration of the mother and, in the depersonalised aspect of the imago, he wants a good reputation for his skills or knowledge in the community. This defusion to competition for a superior reputation in the subject egoistic needs to be complicated, but I'd like to wait for another study to investigate the details of possible adaptations and non-universal aspects.[1] What is important in this study is that the individual appears to have the ontological choice to "make a name for himself" and be his own father or place his name behind the authority of those with Prestige, or who lead a work-group or 'family'. In the former choice, the individual may become a workaholic who 'must' be regarded as more skilled than others, or he may deceptively try to appear as successful by buying status conferring commodities, or by trying to win public opinion by talking about his superiority (Reich, 1990, p. 23, 81, 180; McDougall, 1974, p. 292). However, in these possible defusions, the problem of establishing a phallic father transference to the analyst, one's boss, one's educator, (etc.) is in evidence. They reveal the social ontology of the difference between the generations regarding the pursuit of Prestige in some field of work or the status that is conferred by money, commodities, or membership to certain groups to the image-ego.

Freud's linking of id object cathexis, ego drive, and superego lends itself to a dialectical formulation that suggests that the initial biological tie of the infant to breast supplies a universal ground for the maternal and paternal imagos. There is an id object choice of the mother or, more precisely her finite, material body. Because of the child's inborn instinct for the breast, the parental figure of the finite body will always be associated with the breasted being. When the id object choice is 'instinctually renounced' it then goes on to form ego and object drives for the *in*finite which is a negative quality (i.e., the "not-mother", "not-finite"). The further step is when this perfection becomes linked (through primary identification) to the father who provides symbolic representation through binary logic. The father is, simply, the *not-mother*, otherwise a man wouldn't be capable of recognising a woman as more skilled, intelligent, or potent than himself and transfer authority to a female employer or educator. In the third, synthetic step of the dialectic the ceaseless striving of the ego drive of perfection becomes linked to regulation in culture or what I've taken to calling the higher *social body*. Freud stresses a 'longing for the father' to show the importance of the eros/fusion implicit in the social body that protects one from compulsive ceaseless striving and the ego ideal tension (i.e., inferiority, self-hate) (Freud, 1927, p. 18; 1930, p. 82; 1939, pp. 109–110). From this synthesis it possible to defuse back to the perfection drives related to the negation of the mother. However, I need to point out that this isn't Freud's only use of defusion. Freud (1923b) also links defusion to "the danger of maltreatment and death" from superego (p. 56). I believe this should be considered as a secondary defusion, in what I pointed out in the last chapter as the "need for punishment" in Reich and Fairbairn's formulation of the ego giving itself a lesser, substitutive punishment against a greater fear of the parental imago's punishment.

The dialectic I have outlined is importantly confirmed in the work of Melanie Klein who records the presence of the father (phallus) from the earliest imagos. Klein (1932) also stresses that the perfection associated to the maternal imago by the negation of the finite breast (or object with breasts) is transcribed to the father thus making an underlying 'equation of the breast with the penis' (pp. 213–214). She also goes on to write 'that the frustration [one] has suffered from [the] mother's breast, create in [one] an imaginary picture of [the] father's penis as an organ which, unlike the breast, can provide [one] with a tremendous and never-ending oral gratification (*ibid.*, p. 271). The child would never observe the penis inside the mother's breast or body and therefore these imago relations should never be taken as relying on complex cognition. Rather, the child's own bodily sensations and impulses are imputed to the maternal imago and the paternal imago can be retroactively symbolised once higher stages of development are reached.

II

Just as Freud naturalistically recognises that the finite human mind can't grasp perfection he similarly notes that death is not something that the one can know—as if the soul continues on after death of the body and records the experience (Freud, 1926a, p. 130). It appears as a contradiction when he claims there is a death drive that seeks to return to inorganicity. Although the drives repeat a certain relation, it is only a relation that has already been experienced. He seems to conflate the use of conservation, in saying a drive is the repetition of an earlier state, with the idea that a drive aims at an earlier state which it had not in fact experienced. Id drives like cannibalistic aggression were actually experienced by a child in its psychosexual development and its "primal repression" (creating a fixation) isn't so much an aim to conserve the state so much as the drive functioning as if the state had never changed.[2] When inorganic or inanimate matter becomes animate the previous inanimate state can't be said to have been experienced so Freud's claim of seeking to return to an inorganic state has no relation to the examples of other drives, fish seeking spawn in old waters, nor birds migrations because these relate to states that had previously been experienced (Freud, 1920, p. 37). Although the claim to inorganicity can't hold without un-naturalistically claiming that something in the individual continues to experience after death, the phenomenological state of moving towards tensionlessness is something that can't be disputed. I'll return to it a little later.

The work of Andre Green (1997) on the dead mother has been inspiring. He locates the experience of the mother's death in the passive pole (p. 163), but makes it a contingent experience in which the mother is depressed, mourning, or has a general lack of interest in the child (p. 149). He also goes as far as to put the dead mother as a parallel to the phallic mother which illustrates that it is a "combined parent figure" or non-universal adaptation (ibid., p. 157). However, in doing so Green loses the opportunity to relate this to the drives and merely sees (object altruistic) attempts to rouse, delight, or awaken the object as "reactions of complementarity" that will come to nothing (ibid., p. 151). Additionally, attempts to "repair" the dead mother appear doomed to ambivalence allegedly because there is a thought that, once healthy, she would leave (ibid., 164).

What is needed here is the recognition of defusion *qua* phobos and defusion *qua* need for punishment. The altruist who has defused a second time to the need for punishment may be a "help-rejecting complainer" who is burdened in regard to a sexual relationship (object drives) or in some aspect of her work life (ego drives) but not really trying to get out of the situation. Wurmser (2003) observes the superego punishment in this individuals' torment but also that the individual induces feelings of shame or impotence in the father-substitute for not helping or showing him or her the right way to do things. However, the passive drives in primary defusion (*qua* phobos) can see the altruist helping many people and moving on from relationships instead of being stuck.

Irrespective of what it doesn't do, Green's important essay formalises a parallel principle for development other than perfection that had been in the background of other analysts' work. For example, Jacobson writes of "omnipotent, male-female, breast-phallus figures and castrated, breastless, injured, dead figures" in her work with psychosis (Jacobson, 1954a, p. 254). Additionally, Klein (1975), despite wanting to trace the drive to restore as some kind of reparation for an initial attack, also acknowledges the relation to the mother/not-mother as death. "The reparation tendency too, first employed in an omnipotent way, becomes an important defence," she writes, "the infant's feelings (phantasy) might be described as follows: 'My mother is disappearing, she may never return, she is suffering, she is dead. No, this can't be, for I can revive her'". (ibid., p. 75). I don't think the altruist has to be made responsible for the mother's death as a motivating force for wanting to restore her, nor is a depressed mother necessary for the universal stages. In regard to the latter, the child will always want more than the parents can give, and this inherent excess will be enough to trigger the repression of the id object drives. In regard to the former, why can't aloneness and the desire for oneness with the object or fear of being alone provide a motivation? Klein (1935) was adamant that help and friendliness weren't mere reaction formations but the principle of power again returns into her explanation here (p. 149). This isn't to say that aggression doesn't appear in the altruistic pole because melancholia and masochistic passive-aggression clearly show otherwise. My point here is to not give in to the temptation to compose Eve from Adam's rib in conjectures about depth structures, when phemomenology points to a different experience.

III

While the egoist identifies with the perfection that comes to be linked to the father imago, and feels an imperative to be perfect, the self is experienced differently for the altruist. Instead of mere egoism through a proxy, the formulation of Horney (1937), following Nietzsche, is more substantive. The principle of individuation is associated with active-egoism while the Dionysian principle of an ecstatic experience in oneness comprises the other pole (p. 270). Instead of the egoistic power binary of on top/on the bottom, there is a "participation mystique" in oneness with the group and the binary of inside/outside. While the altruist retains union with the group, difference or separation enters in the form of the object being outside of the group—literally being an outsider—and its need to be restored to the inside. This can either be interpreted as compassion for a sibling or the idealisation of the leader who must be restored, just as the egoistic can compete with siblings or the leader of the group.

However, these two starting principles can't remain so simple and untroubled. Despite Klein's disposition for interpreting the surface with an egoistic depth model, she still has impressive phenomenological observations to share that make her depth models more than just ordering abstractions. The most important model for the opposition between egoism and altruism came from her insight that the two poles slowly begin to mix in development. Klein writes:

> I have pointed out elsewhere that in the quite small child there exists, side by side with its relations to real objects- but on a different plane, as it were—relations to its unreal imagos, both as excessively good [passive-altruism] and excessively bad figures [active-egoism], and that these two kinds of object-relations intermingle and colour each other to an ever-increasing degree in the course of development. The first important steps in this direction occur, in my view, when the child comes to know its mother as a whole person and becomes identified with her as a whole, real and loved person. (Klein, 1935, p. 171)

The intermingling of the imagos, "to an ever-increasing degree in the course of development", is important in making sense of several concepts. As I mentioned in Chapter One, Klein and Reich have suggested, a person may not develop both poles to the same extent. If the phallic egoistic drives weren't formed in an individual then there would be no way to make sense of the self-assertion concerning the image-ego that does show up in these altruists. Additionally, as I'll get to, the egoistic wouldn't be capable of the aggressive drive of wanting to kill or bring death to the father because he couldn't have experienced death himself and any intellectual construction of it would be far off.

The intermingling of the two poles, as I hinted last chapter appears to reach its culmination in the father complex. I could understand how someone might argue that social narcissism in latency is a fuller expression of altruism in the egoistic pole, but the important hallmarks of altruism are there at the father-complex. When the subject egoistic establishes *social feeling* and wants to be recognised as an "adult" for his fairness and manners and forms a guilt conscience of equality with other persons/citizens, the striving for magnification of the self appears tempered. Here the on top/on bottom and the inside/outside binaries both seem applicable. However, phenomenologically, the subject egoist's self-observation of "duty", which is formed after the father complex, is different from the "devotion" of the subject altruist, and the two wouldn't be confused by people with good judgment. Before this stage, as I noted above, Freud observes the solidarity in a work group that is brought about by fusion with a father-substitute. This can be taken as a preliminary form of the intermingling before the balance is reached in the father complex. Additionally, in the first chapter I showed that Freud saw love as an oedipal development for the egoistic after earlier interest in satisfying sexual infatuation or what I've aligned with possessing or controlling the object is superseded.

A neat parallel to subject egoistic development is suggested by the work of Chasseguet-Smirgel in the female Oedipus complex. In "Female sexuality" Freud (1931a) designates the Oedipus complex "to include all the child's relations to both parents" or triangular relationships in general (p. 226). Although I believe that other myths are better at describing the phallic nuclear complexes for the different libidinal positions, I will wait for another project to bring them into play and retain the oedipal designation for the subject altruist. Additionally, I also use the term castration complex to refer to all defused, triangular relationships that aren't derived from a primal scene. Freud's contrast of the boy's castration complex with the girl's fear of loss of love does have an important phenomenological difference that I will cover, but the structural relation to the father-substitute is where the importance of the phallus comes from (Freud, 1933, pp. 87–88). Additionally, women have been noted to have castration anxiety as early as Abraham (1922) so I don't see the need to be as anatomical as Freud does.

Chasseguet-Smirgel, in an important article on the female Oedipus and castration complexes, lays out the phenomenological plane, along with depth phantasies, for the subject altruist. Her general view is that self-assertion becomes problematic for altruists and that secondary roles are the drive-based lot of altruistic women. Chasseguet-Smirgel (1970) writes:

basically, penis envy is the symbolic expression of another desire. Women do not wish to become men, but want to detach themselves from the mother and become complete, autonomous women. (Chasseguet-Smirgel, 1970, p. 118)

Far from being autonomous with regard to the object, she is closely dependent on it and is also its complement. She is the right hand, the assistant, the colleague, the secretary, the auxiliary, the inspiration for an employer, a lover, a husband, a father. She may also be a companion for old age, guide, or nurse. One sees the basic conflicts underlying such relationships in clinical practice. (ibid., p. 124)

Acting for oneself, being autonomous, creating for oneself meant possessing the paternal penis and thus castrating the father (ibid., p. 128)

I would readily see this as the source of one of woman's main conflicts, that of being relative to men, just as nearly all of woman's cultural or social achievements are. Women are said to produce few original works; they are often the brilliant disciple of a man or of a masculine theory. They are rarely leaders of movements. This is surely the effect of a conflict specific to women. (ibid., p. 131)

Just as the subject egoistic defuses from the oedipal father imago to become competitive with friends and bosses, the subject altruist loses the ability to be assertive and her restorative drives come to the fore in "auxillary" positions. In the first chapter I noted that object egoistic and subject altruistic positions help to understand the different forms of penis envy that have been described by various analysts and the one described here aligns with the subject altruistic position. Chasseguet-Smirgel's insight into the subject altruist doesn't mean that all pre-genital women are this way. Additionally, since subject egoism is aligned with musculature, it is only a matter of probability that human males are more often subject egoists; there are women who are predominately subject egoistic in regards to their libidinal positions.

Regardless of the sexed phantasies that may underpin the libidinal positions, what is important in this investigation is the observable behaviour. The *respect* that the subject egoistic has for the father-substitute is lost in defusion, to be replaced by mere *respect for self*, while the *self-loyalty* of the subject altruist in fusion with the father becomes only *loyalty* to others and their hopes. Respect for self alone in the subject egoistic will lead to the experience of tension in *inferiority* that is associated with the imperative to be one's own father. In the subject altruist, Chasseguet-Smirgel uses part-object language to describe the fear of castrating the father when he or she acts "for oneself" or "autonomously". However, Karen Horney (1950) gives a much better phenomenological description so that we can pair loyalty feelings with tensions of feeling presumptuousness, selfishness, greediness, etc., that can all generally be labelled as *conceit* (p. 54). The restorative impulses themselves are paired with loyalty as the function of the ego ideal. "Loyalty is more than an ordinary bond, more than an 'object relationship'" Leon Wurmser (1988) writes, "it sets up the other as a beloved authority over oneself toward whom one has to keep faith. It is a kind of superego relationship and superego bond" (Wurmser, 1988, p. 387). The castration complex in the subject altruist concerns the castration of the object who becomes the outsider. In the social realm the passive struggle to help less fortunate others—to help outsiders become insiders—is in evidence, while the loyalty to a specific person may mean that the altruist tries to assist his or her striving for perfection. In the first chapter this was discussed in the forms of taking up skills or knowledge the partner lacks, devoting oneself to carry on the object's work or keeping their name prominent, or living their way of life and honouring them through this. However, as noted there, some of this comes from defensive operation against loss of the object.

To return to the subject egoistic, it is important to stress, that although the guilt conscience and feelings of equality with others don't enter until the father complex, this doesn't mean he can't be preoccupied with morality. Nietzsche (1974) has a very keen eye for how morality often shows up as a form of establishing one's superiority and not from felt equality:

> there is a human being who has turned out badly, who does not have enough spirit to be able to enjoy it but just enough education to realize this; he is bored, disgusted, and despises himself; having inherited some money, he is deprived even of the last comfort, "the blessings of work," self-forgetfulness in "daily labour." Such a person who is fundamentally ashamed of his existence—perhaps he also harbours a few little vices—and on the other hand cannot keep himself from becoming more and more spoiled and irritable by reading books to which he is not entitled or by associating with

more spiritual company than he can digest ... for spirit becomes
poison, education becomes poison, possessions become poison,
solitude becomes poison for those who have turned out badly in
this way—eventually [he] ends up in a state of habitual revenge,
will to revenge ... what do you suppose he finds necessary, absolutely necessary, to give himself in his own eyes the appearance of
superiority over more spiritual people and to attain the pleasure of
an *accomplished revenge* at least in his imagination? Always *morality*;
you can bet on that. Always big moral words. Always the rub-a-
dub of justice, wisdom, holiness, virtue. Always the stoicism of gesture (how well Stoicism conceals what one lacks!). Always the cloak
of prudent silence, of affability, of mildness, and whatever may be
the names of all the other idealistic cloaks in which incurable self-
despisers, as well as the incurably vain, strut about ... (Nietzsche,
1974, p. 314)

Here Nietzsche expresses his intuition that failure in success can be
cloaked in morality. In the last chapter the "social anxiety" of the pre-
genital subject egoistic was discussed. His desire to have the reputation of being moral was somewhat caricatured as purely instrumental
(i.e., a moral reputation is good for business) and that so long as others
didn't find out, he had no problem being immoral. In Nietzsche's picture
we still wouldn't say the subject egoistic is lying and merely pretending to espouse morality. Rather, once we acknowledge that wanting to
appear moral isn't the same as feeling equal to others, nor possessing the
guilt conscience, we can go beyond pure instrumentality to say that the
subject egoistic at the phallic stage is driven to want to appear moral.

Because of the intermingling of the two poles, the descriptions of both
the subject egoistic and altruist need to be rounded out by noting two
more tensions in the superego. Additionally, this allows me to get rid
of the redundancy of passive-altruistic in order to say that this desire to
appear moral or honourable could be called active-altruism. Moreover,
as I mentioned in Chapter Two, the idea of being able to make promises,
although non-moral, could conceivably be linked to moral ideas to create active-masochism in some instances. However, what is much more
common is hypocrisy, denial, and projection, and, though my personal
clinical experience doesn't give me many examples of it, an ego ideal
of tension that compliments the striving for the image of goodness is
evidenced in something like feeling phoney, or like a fraud.

To complement this, the subject altruist, in being driven to love and be kind to others, can encounter a lot of mistreatment with a response that can resemble being egoistic. However, passive-egoism will never appear as the ambition, need for admiration for one's abilities, etc. as it does in the egoistic, just as affability, mildness, and sweetness can only be a thin veneer in active-altruism. Additionally, the goal of perfection is sometimes more explicit in passive-egoism than it is in active-egoism. However, the perfectionism and "hard-working" aspect is clearly joined up with wanting to be seen as such by the father-substitutes at the job site and there is anxiety about disappointing them. Even to the extent that this is eclipsed by some surliness, for those who can't see past this "grumpy" cloak, the altruist's behaviour in the work group will still give him away.

Just as traversing the father complex leads to the egoistic feeling equality with other adults in the community instead of being concerned with personal success or love, it establishes the altruist's ability to be equal in regards to pursuing her self-interest. In the father complex, the subject altruist develops guilt in relation to her self-assertion, "owing it to herself to be more", and wanting to be on top. Here the altruist would consider being a work group leader, but in the passive-egoism of the castration complex there would be no striving for leadership. As passive phallic "devotion" becomes greatly softened to active genital "duty", the sense of active phallic "glory" for which the subject egoistic strives becomes softened to striving for passive "glamour". The pop culture phenomenon of "bridezillas", for example, illustrates that a subject altruist can get past the castration complex tensions of conceit and effacement of her own desires, and when it comes to her "adult" wedding she can become quite assertive about what she wants and how things have to be.

There are subtle phenomenological distinctions at work in word choices. It should be apparent that at the Oedipus complex there is already a strong intermixing of the two poles and what many people of poor judgement use as synonyms actually contain important differences that betray libidinal economy with its various drives, defences, and deficits. So, to contrast the active tension of inferiority that implies the comparison with someone who is superior, the more global connotation of inadequacy seems more apt for the subject altruist's passive-egoism. Lastly, to be clear, active-altruism in the egoistic and passive-egoism in the altruist don't arise merely from some defensive operation. The example from Nietzsche and the cynical altruist were chosen in order to exaggerate the functioning of the cross-bred drive.

IV

Perfection and Death become apparent in the operation of what Klein calls projective identification. Klein (1975) writes of an operation in which both the bad and hated parts of the self, as well as the good parts too, are projected into the object (p. 8). It is an ego defence and as such, concerns the management of anxiety, although Klein also holds that it can cause new anxiety situations as well (ibid., p. 166fn). The inferiority tensions in the subject egoistic are coupled with his aggressive id impulses that cause anxiety when directed at the parental imago. When the self imago exchanges places with the parental imago, the anxiety and inferiority tensions are projected into the object who now occupies the self imago. However, by assuming perfection "and expelling into the outer world parts of itself [the individual is] considerably weaken[ed]," Klein writes, "for the aggressive component of feelings and of the personality is intimately bound up in the mind with power, potency, strength, knowledge and many other desired qualities ... and in this way the mother [imago] becomes the ego-ideal" (Klein, 1975, p. 8). In other words, to switch places with the parental imago of perfection means that one no longer strives for perfection under the demands of the ego ideal because one *is* perfection. Similarly, when the subject altruist exchanges places with death, she puts her ego ideal tensions and the anxiety paired with affection in the other person. I think that anyone who works with substance abuse will feel altruistic projective identification with death very often. I've worked with many women who place altruistic tensions and anxieties into their families or lovers as they throw their reputation away and fall through the cracks of society in their drug use.

Projective identification with death and the move towards its tensionlessness enters into earlier levels of Being. In the next section I'll enter into an investigation of how to conceptualise this pluralistic ontology, but for now it's apparent that in perfection, for example, one can falsely believe that one is important and talked about by others in the community and that this can be increased all the way to megalomania. In a primitive level of Being the move towards tensionlessness can be revealed in the body itself before the ego drives and ideal reference the permanency of social hierarchy. Eigen (1995) gives an example of a patient who manifested this relation in her body's loss of vitality and its skeletal quality. In "aping [death], by becoming its proxy" he writes "her skeleton rips the eyes of the Other, tears the Other's heart" (Eigen, 1995, pp. 280–282). The client's lack of vitality and wasting away on the path of losing tension, calls up Freud's phenomenological observation of why a death drive was postulated and offers another route for its explanation that stays true to his original principles. It is difficult to tell if Green (1997) was talking about the reaction of aloneness as the white depression behind the black depression of melancholic self-reproaches or if he saw the projective identification with death without noting his own countertransference. To my eye, so long as there is the renewed tension of aloneness or the energetic self-reproach of melancholia then there is a clear difference with the slackening of tension involved in projective identification.

Although projective identification is contested by many, it doesn't significantly differ from the operation of turning an injury one has received into something one perpetrates on others (turning passive to active *qua* defence). Instead of a specific injury it is more general anxiety that is given to the object. In Freud's (1920) example of repetition-compulsions in which a woman marries several men who die and a mentor is betrayed by his proteges multiple times, anxiety is clearly being sought out through unconscious channels. So, why can't the person causing anxiety in these repetitions not similarly unconsciously sense others who will receive his or her anxiety and allow him to play the role of parental imago? However, this is mostly a matter of owning up to objective countertransference feelings. If one is embarrassed of how one's patients make one feel, doesn't function in the altruistic pole, or doesn't feel in general, then this won't be recognised.

Lastly, it's important to bear in mind that this naturalistic conception of perfection and the loyalty to another in their death is partially *extrinsic* to objects (people) or things. This means that overtop of the libidinal positions having their own ego and object drives and different versions of beauty, the good life or politics, love, etc. that there are also individual differences among subject egoists, for example. There is individual maturation to be recognised. It is obvious that the wrestler who the subject-egoistic child judges as perfect in primary school may seem less than perfect to him at the end of secondary school where a more complexly motivated or intellectual idol might take his place. Again, this is more than culturally determined and we can look back to the Greeks to see a physically powerful Hercules and then a more sophisticated Odysseus. I don't have conceptual tools to address individual maturation but if it is to be trans-historical then it must be part of the drives. A likely candidate would be the tension between the active-egoistic and passive altruistic poles creating higher syntheses, as symbolically recognised by Jung (1944) in his work on alchemy and individuation. Maturation is more than being filled with knowledge from one's historical political-economy. Insights have to be won in order to give this information meaning and feel it imbue one's perception with significance.

V

Although Freud's work has a coherent framework for the genesis of perfection and its relation to the image-ego drives and parental imagos, the important question is how we can conceive of the earlier forms of perfection? Freud did have the hope to go beyond the reference to the phallic image-ego when he wrote, "it may be expected that when we penetrate deeper into the psychology of the psychoses [the superego's] significance will be discovered to be far greater" (Freud, 1921, p. 130). However, psychoanalysis didn't develop that way. Klein, Fairbairn, and others studied the pre-phallic forms of the superego and the different imagos that contributed to them but without much focus on their characterological implications. In American psychoanalysis, just as Kohut was introducing pre-oedipal forms of transference that might have united the continental with the American schools, he began distancing himself from Freud's metaphsychology. "Adultomorphism", as a concept that holds that the child doesn't have the cognitive capacities in pre-oedipal development to form ideational content to influence character, was used against the continental schools and classical psychoanalysis (Kohut, 1971, pp. 37–38, 220). Classical theory with its "impressionistic" ideas about character being formed by the child's judging its relations to archaic forms of the parents' omnipotence was rejected. A great example of this, to which I'll return, is Edmund Bergler's concept of the artist:

> according to my conception, the writer's type of neurotic orality is not greediness and a wish to "get" in the repetition of the child–mother situation, but rather a spiteful desire for oral

> independence, whereby the artist identifies himself with the "giving" mother out of aggression toward her, and thus eliminates her. He achieves oral pleasures for himself through "beautiful" words and ideas. In its deepest sense, it is a desire to refute the "bad" pre-oedipal mother and the disappointments experienced through her, by establishing an "autarchy". (Bergler, 1944, p. 46)

In Bergler's example the infant at the breast is somehow able to spite the "giving mother" with beautiful words and ideas by establishing an autarchy that refutes her omnipotence. I agree with the assessment that the emotion of spite and forming judgements on the beauty of words seem much too sophisticated for the infant.[3] However, I'd like a return to Freud's metapsychology in order to systematise some of the insights of classical psychoanalysis along the lines of social ontology and show that there was some truth in these impressionsistic formulations. The key is that the adultomporphic criticism has been lodged against the pre-phallic superego because an atomistic view of the individual has been assumed. However, as I argued, Freud doesn't base perfection upon the child observing and processing complicated relationships of power, but on an underlying primary relatedness. This relatedness is usually referred to, rather bitterly, as the child's "helplessness" and supplies the causation for why the child would direct its aggression inward and introject the parental imago (Freud, 1930, p. 123). What Freud's superego offers is a social ontology that places individual character not in the child grasping complicated relations but in the necessity of both the mind and reality being created intersubjectively through internalisation of parental imagos. This has to be understood on two levels. The first is the simple observation that despite shared social conventions for measuring time and space an individual has a subject sense of them and can feel time dragging on or going by quickly or marvel at how small his childhood bedroom seems when he returns to it as an adult. The second is to recognise the importance of Kant's Copernican revolution in epistemology—a revolution that need not be presented in so complicated and convoluted manner, as I will show.

As I mentioned in the last chapter, Freud did move general reality-testing from the superego to the ego *qua* perceptual consciousness system, but the idea of the ego ideal as measuring the ego living up to the demands for perfection is a different—a social sense—of reality. The performance of the ego is measured against the performance of others and the egoistic experiences inferiority (tension between the ego and ego ideal) when he is "outclassed" by another in competition or another's superior Prestige reveals his failure to measure up. This is different than the perception and reality testing that concerns regular epistemology, which is often based on much more mundane things, such as how one knows that there is or is not a chair in the room or how many coins one has in his pocket. One must keep social or intersubjective reality, and its relation to a philosophy of action that is drive and superego based, apart from regular perception of items in the environment.

Freud's discussions of the pleasure and reality principle are claims based upon drive motivation and therefore concern social reality. Again, this "reality" is dependent upon one's functioning libidinal positions. The more libidinal positions functioning, and the more their conflict has pushed for higher syntheses, the more social reality one can perceive. In the first chapter I suggested that some religious constructs, like yin and yang for example, were more than just irrationality or phantasy and might show that beyond perception of distinct character attributes and motivations, that there is an understanding of connections between these phenomena. I'm sure that this maturation *qua* individuation also affects understanding and creativity in the "hard" sciences—beyond mere memorisation—but it's outside of my scope to enter into this.

Freud's work "Formulations on the two principles of mental functioning" (1911a) concerns this concept of social reality in relation to imagos. "A system living according to the pleasure principle must have devices to enable it to withdraw from the stimuli of reality" Freud writes; "such devices are merely the correlative of 'repression,' which treats internal unpleasurable stimuli as if they were external—that is to say, pushes them into the external world" (ibid., p. 219). This means that there are many "systems" grouped around the superego and its measurement of the performance of the individual that are attached to some reality sense. Each of these systems must allow for the individual to withdraw from measurement of ego performance in relation to others and enter into defences like paranoia. In paranoia unpleasurable self-criticism in the ego ideal returns in the form of the father imago's watchful persecution that allows the active-egoistic to retain some self-esteem after a narcissistic injury, but at the cost of perverting social reality (Freud, 1914b, p. 102). In melancholia, depression, as the introjection of the father's badness, conserves the ability of the passive-altruist to vouchsafe her source of self-esteem too. To understand the latter process Fairbairn (1952) spells out the logic in his statement "it is better to be a sinner in a world ruled by God than to live in a world ruled by the Devil" (Fairbairn, 1952, pp. 66–67). Since the transference to the father-substitute involves the functioning of the reality principle *qua* social reality, the frustrations induced by the father-substitute would make the relations of Prestige, at the phallic level, seem evil and unable to give the approval that the altruist needs. The melancholic, takes on the blame (perverts inner reality) and attacks herself in order to save her outer reality, just as the paranoiac perverts outer reality to save the self-esteem that comes from his inner reality and agency.

Along with the psychodynamics of defences, neurotic illusions that aren't played out in the relationship of superego to ego exist in the repetition-compulsions of both social (ego drive) and sexual (object drive) relationships (Freud, 1921, p. 130). These repetition-compulsions of the pleasure principle offer the promise of great satisfaction, as noted above in Klein's description of "tremendous and never-ending oral gratification". Although they don't twist reality so noticeably as paranoia does, the implicit idealisation of the ego or object's abilities or worth is an illusion. These illusions, as we've seen, are based upon the drive's negative existence and also still reference the father-imago in defused rivalry with a father-substitute. Narcissistic triumph may result in intense pleasure as the incest taboo/difference between the generations is crossed in a social or sexual relationship but it loses its lustre. Witticisms such as "I don't want to belong to a club that would have me as a member" illustrate the sense of betrayed illusion once one attains a goal. Happiness was supposed to follow when one got the girl or job one wanted, but it didn't stay.

In the last chapter, and revisited above, I argued that Freud differentiates the guilt conscience that is formed after the Oedipus complex, in the father complex, from the social anxiety achieved in the Oedipus complex. Freud (1930) writes that at the Oedipus complex:

> the sense of guilt is clearly only a fear of loss of love, "social" anxiety. In small children it can never be anything else, but in many adults, too, it has only changed to the extent that the place of the father or the two parents is taken by the larger human community. Consequently, such people habitually allow themselves to do any

bad thing which promises them enjoyment, so long as they are sure
that the authority will not know anything about it or cannot blame
them for it; they are afraid only of being found out. (Freud, 1930,
pp. 124–125)

In another place Freud refers to the authorities in "the larger human
community" taking on the oedipal parent's power as "the *depersonali-
zation* of the parental agency" (Freud, 1926a, p. 139, emphasis mine).
Freud doesn't use this term in relation to the other imagos of the superego but his work suggests three earlier forms from which I'll begin my
investigation of the different forms of perfection and death.

The earliest form of imago depersonalisation comes from *Civilization and Its Discontents* (1930) in Freud's discussion of oceanic oneness,
which he describes as

> a feeling of an indissoluble bond, of being one with the external
> world as a whole .... originally the ego includes everything, later it
> separates off an external world from itself. Our present ego-feeling
> is, therefore, only a shrunken residue of a much more inclusive—
> indeed, an all-embracing—feeling which corresponded to a more
> intimate bond between the ego and the world about it. If we may
> assume that there are many people in whose mental life this pri-
> mary ego-feeling has persisted to a greater or less degree, it would
> exist in them side by side with the narrower and more sharply
> demarcated ego-feeling of maturity, like a kind of counterpart to
> it. In that case, the ideational contents appropriate to it would be
> precisely those of limitlessness and of a bond with the universe—
> the same ideas with which my friend elucidated the "oceanic" feel-
> ing ... . the oceanic feeling, which might seek something like the
> restoration of limitless narcissism. (Freud, 1930, pp. 65, 68, 72)

Freud holds that the connection of the ego with the world begins with
the "infant at the breast" who doesn't distinguish itself from the external world. The reality principle already enters very early as the infant
is responsible for "deliberate direction of ... sensory activities and ...
muscular action ... [to] differentiate between what is internal ... and
what is external" (ibid., p. 67). While the phallic father has its depersonalised dimension in the Prestige and accreditation that conveys his
authority, the establishment of what is internal and external requires
a depersonalised dimension that can best be described as Space. This

has important ties to Freud's concept of phantasy. In Freud's view, the infant, following the pleasure principle, first satisfies his desire for the breast as either social contact with the caregiver or in hunger, in the form of hallucinated mnemic traces. This hallucinated satisfaction however, must give way to some contact with reality so that infant can "refind" the mnemic traces in the field of external, reality (Freud, 1925, p. 237). From the confusion of internal and external, comes the establishment of external Space. Since a break in the mind can allow the two to become confused again in hallucination, this reality sense can be conceptualised as a relation to a depersonalised parental imago. As such, an individual with a fixation at this point in development may feel the primitive aggression called up in the hate he feels in more complex social or sexual relationships. If the fixated aggression feels too overwhelming, then the relation to the primitive imago will be defended against so that phantasy and reality may be confused.

The position that Time and Space are conditions of the perception of things that must have their own subjective aspect that is produced by the mind, was first introduced by the philosopher Kant (1999). His position is different from the previous forms of philosophical idealism that solipsistically hold that the external world might just "be in one's head". He requires that the mind's faculties must first be awakened by external reality and doesn't allow that God could have already given us innate ideas about the world (Kant, 1999, "The refutation of idealism"). Although Kant doesn't avail himself of the existence of dreaming in his argument, the fact that we dream proves that there is an internal sense of Space and Time that isn't just simply caused by stimuli in the external world. Moreover, if a philosopher might wonder how we can tell dreaming apart from being awake, the erratic change of location, sense of time, and the people and things in a dream, along with the suspension of the qualitative processes that accompany linear experience make this possible.

There have been interpreters that argue that Kant refutes objective or noumenal time or space and lump him with the simple idealism he criticises or intends to refute. However, in the refutation of idealism Kant (1999) is explicit that there is a noumenal world that causes our perceptions even though we don't have access to it "in itself". If the permanence of the noumenal world can't be quantified in time then it makes no sense to refute the earlier idealists who claim that it is possible that God gives them the perceptions of the external world and it is only in their minds. To be clear, the subjective sense of Time is a different thing altogether from the development of cognition in later stages that allows one to use arithmetic and the established social conventions of time measurement and numerical bases that allow objective time to be established. Ultimately, Freud deepens the Kantian position to further show the necessity of the intersubjective in the creation of the mind and the social ontology that is derived from parental imagos and manifested through pathological breaks with (social) reality.

As with the phallic castration complex, Freud himself brings up the idea of a corresponding anxiety to this transference to the world *qua* Space. In the former defusion from the father imago, "making a name for oneself" can result in anxiety-laden encounters with would-be father-substitutes who want to attack one's reputation or threaten to "steal" one's love object (causing the death of the egoist's image-ego). In the latter, the father-substitute exists in the form of a transference that can generally be described as feeling secure in the world in general. Importantly, Klein (1948) indicates, the real, externally caused anxiety brought on by the bombings in World War Two registered changes in the imago relations of her patients (p. 122). Clearly the infant can't have a perception of the world, and Freud registers this concern. He raises the idea that the anxiety of "falling out of the world", which the work of certain artists suggests, is adultomorphic, or has "the nature of an intellectual perception" that an adult would have (Freud, 1930, p. 65). However, where the sign or word-presentation of "the world" surely indicates advanced cognition, what is at stake here is a retroactive link of "the world", and in advanced political-economies, the solar system and universe with the depersonalised imago of Space. Falling anxiety need only reference the subjective sense of Space, and then its negation, while the intellectual content can change so that the world is conceived of as being flat, on a turtle's back, round and in the centre of the universe, part of a solar system, etc.

Castration anxiety and the depersonalisation of Space can be presented in several ways and future research will have to link them to the libidinal positions. Analysts such as W. Reich, Tustin, and Grotstein have considered falling anxiety, falling into infinite space, or into a "black hole", or "spilling away" to be the first (post birth) anxiety situation (Grotstein, 1990, pp. 381–382; Reich, 1973a, p. 346; 1983, pp. 114–135; Tustin, 1988, pp. 40–42). However, I'm skeptical of claims that imago relations earlier than the ones Klein investigated have come to light. Instead, I think that egoistic and altruistic positions have different phantasies and erotogenic zones. The reference to oceanic oneness with the father imago is clearly an altruistic reference to the world. However, I'm not sure if falling anxiety is a reaction to feeling one is alone in the world or if it is a new anxiety situation brought about by projective identification.

A subject egoistic relation might be closer to wanting to annihilate Space (the world) and fear of one's own annihilation. Establishing the id forms of aggression and affection and their related anxiety are very important for certain clinical techniques, but I am unable to do more than offer hypotheses here under the rubric of psychic bisexuality. At least, Klein (1975) holds the earliest destructive drive is one of "maximal sadism" that becomes reduced as it is synthesised with the "life drives" or intermingled with the altruistic pole (p. 92). Additionally, more recent research, like in the work of Tustin (1984) indicates interesting pre-Space "autistic shapes" and McDougall (1989b) establishes the archaic dialectical relation between mind and body that allows for somato-psychic illnesses. However, entering into different forms of the ego's perceptual-consciousness and all the types of symptoms isn't possible either. The most I can do here is sketch the more general levels of Being for perfection and death as a groundwork for future investigations.

The relation of depersonalisation to the world *qua* Space in which the mnemic traces are refound there is designated as the auto-erotic stage by Freud. Bergler's conception of the artist can be rehabilitated as rivalry with the depersonalised father of external Space. The artist in the act of creating art is not refinding his mnemic traces in the external world but rather offering a substitute world for someone to look upon or, by using words, to enter through the "mind's eye". The artist, and probably any intellectual, is someone who displays the ontological choice between giving their attention to their phantasy or internal mnemic traces or the external world and the mnemic traces refound there. Freud (1917b) writes:

> an artist is once more in rudiments an introvert, not far removed from neurosis. He is oppressed by excessively powerful instinctual needs. He desires to win honour, power, wealth, fame and the love of women; but he lacks the means for achieving these satisfactions. Consequently, like any other unsatisfied man, he turns away from reality and transfers all his [ego] interest, and his [object] libido too, to the wishful constructions of his life of phantasy, whence the path might lead to neurosis. (Freud, 1917b, p. 375)

In this passage, Freud gives the most general formulation of sublimation that doesn't reference a particular impulse. It involves the idea that the reputation seeking ego drives and love seeking object drives of the phallic stage can be rerouted back to the earlier ideal of phantasy in the auto-erotic stage. This isn't a simple process and requires that the phallic ideal be kept alive and not defended against. All the feelings (based upon drives, father-substitutes, peer rivals, etc.) in the phallic level of Being have to be captured without the artist letting his individual complexes get the upper hand. Additionally, art isn't a reference to phantasy alone and to create new forms, or have his originality of form recognised, the artist must be aware of conventions and know how to break them. Although there are many elaborations from other reality/Being systems, the initial opposition between the individual's own phantasy world and external reality does follow Bergler's insight. The artist is creating his own autarchy of possible worlds that are comprised of mnemic traces that protest being found in the external world *qua* perceptions in Space.

Freud introduced his concept of narcissism by the examination of pathology. In "On narcissism" Freud (1914b) explicates the concept based upon the observation that psychotic and physically sick people can be reduced to a state in which they lose their motivations to strive for power, find a sexual object, (etc.). He writes:

> closer observation teaches us that he [the sick man] also withdraws libidinal interest from his love-objects: so long as he suffers, he ceases to love. The commonplace nature of this fact is no reason why we should be deterred from translating it into terms of the libido theory. We should then say: the sick man withdraws his libidinal cathexes back upon his own ego, and sends them out again when he recovers. "Concentrated is his soul," says Wilhelm Busch of the poet suffering from toothache, "in his molar's narrow hole." *Here libido and ego-interest share the same fate and are once more indistinguishable from each other*. The familiar egoism of the sick person covers both. We find it so natural because we are certain that in the same situation we should behave in just the same way. (Freud, 1914b, pp. 82–83, emphasis mine)

In these examples the later ego ideals aren't rererouted back to the ego ideal of phantasy. Rather, the energy that goes to later ideals is simply kept back to give more of it to the process of physical healing (in the sick person) or the later ideals are defended against (in the psychotic person). The sick person will move the energy back once the illness has been beaten but the psychotic person can't move his energy back unless the defences against the later ideals are lowered with some help. Freud doesn't claim that the child, psychotic, or ill person isn't aware of objects, as many contemporary psychoanalysts criticise him for. If we follow his example the psychotic and sick person surely perceive and interact with others. Rather, the claim is that the "demands for perfection" experienced in later forms of the superego are not receiving any energy and don't motivate the individual. Again, at the extreme one can witness a psychotic person who is content to sit around and smoke without any social interaction. He, along with the child going through this stage, are aware of others through the perceptual consciousness system, but, as far as the ego is concerned the only drives at this stage are auto-erotic drives that aren't measured in the sense of demanding comparison to others. Freud (1926a) suggests that the perceptual-consciousness system as a modification of the id comes into existence before birth so that birth itself becomes an important anxiety situation. However, there is an important stage of secondary narcissism in which the ego and object drives are differentiated by a "demand for perfection" that measures them in relation to others in the external world so that the ego and object drives are distinguishable from one another (Freud, 1914b, 1923b, p. 46).

In the next stage of the ego ideal, which Freud calls the narcissistic stage, the measurement of the ideal demanding perfection based upon an enduring comparison with others is still not established. Rather, as Freud (1911b) suggest, it is a "half-way phase":

> recent investigations have directed our attention to a stage in the development of the libido which it passes through on the way from auto-erotism to object-love. This stage has been given the name of narcissism. What happens is this. There comes a time in the development of the individual at which he unifies his sexual instincts (which have hitherto been engaged in auto-erotic activities) in order to obtain a love-object; and he begins by taking himself, his own body, as his love-object, and only subsequently proceeds from this to the choice of some person other than himself as his object. This half-way phase between auto-erotism and object-love may perhaps

be indispensable normally; but it appears that many people linger unusually long in this condition, and that many of its features are carried over by them into the later stages of their development. (Freud, 1911b, pp. 60–61)

Before the discussion of the depersonalisation of the father imago and the ontological choice between the (social) reality and pleasure principle, the adultomorphic representation of this stage has to be addressed. Freud (1913) compares this stage of development to animism and claims that the child ascribes omnipotence to itself (p. 88). However, Freud doesn't substantiate this claim and it contradicts his positing the reality principle at each stage and the necessity of recognising the father imago's power (i.e., what at the phallic oedipal is recognised as the difference between the generations). Keeping with Freud's naturalistic approach, there can't be any "innate idea" regarding perfection. This means that the child can only ascribe power to itself after it has recognised the perception of power externally in something else. As we've seen, this occurs partially in the egoistic taking back respect for the father imago to increase his respect for self and, if the egoist doesn't feel like he has to prove himself in some way, then projective identification is in order.

Freud (1909) does possess a softer claim about omnipotence in the narcissistic stage that concerns not the omnipotence of the child but, rather, the omnipotence of thoughts, which still possesses a vital insight. From the realm of phantasy in which the mnemic traces of external objects are rearranged in one's mind's eye, this "limitless narcissism" becomes "primary narcissism" and concerns "the omnipotence of thoughts, or, more accurately" Freud writes, "of wishes" (p. 235). Instead of the "made up" internal world of phantasy, these wishes concern objects existing in the external world. Pleasure is found in the feeling that one's love, hate, and desire for power or restoration actually affects objects and things in the external world. It is the feeling that one's hate can behave like an "evil eye" and cause death to someone, that by picturing one's success in one's mind, that this success will be manifested in the external world, and that one can control or summon an object with one's mind. As indicated above, Klein also noted wishes to restore the object that are omnipotent in this soft sense, and many new age healers believe they can send healing energies to others who are many hours away from them. Thus magic, the ability to fly or possesses psychic powers, and many mystical doctrines are examples of this magical thinking or omnipotent wishing. Many people suffering from psychosis also display the omnipotence of wishes and speak of the good luck they bring people, their sexual magnetism, or magical abilities. Freud (1919b) also mentions several examples of the magical thinking at this stage under the rubric of the uncanny.

In the narcissistic stage the father imago in its depersonalised form is best described as Time. Time is what is needed to see if one's wishes actually have an effect on the object. In castration complex rivalry with Time one's intentions alone are felt to have power and the ontological choice is between giving power to one's wishes or giving power to action that shows its efficacy. The transference to Time is embodied in an external person and in the castration complex the father imago threatens to devour or swallow one up. I have to point out the children's game "What Time is it Mr. Wolf" in which Time and being eaten are so intimately related.[4] For a long time the mouth is the most coordinated part of the bodily musculature and provides several forms of aggression in different stages. Therefore it is important to pay attention to the qualitative difference between biting, swallowing, devouring or gobbling, (etc.). Although cannibals eat another person, the mythological representation of Cronos having his children in his body, or Jonah being whole in the whale, suggests that aggression at this stage isn't so much in the act of chewing and biting as it is in incorporation.

The "castration" fear at these different stages is a fear that ultimately must be linked to projection as Klein points out (Klein, 1975, p. 30). It's not that the parents actually threaten to swallow the child whole, but the child would like to blot out the perception of the father's power and have it for himself and it projects this impulse upon the father imago. The musculature of the mouth happens to be the locus of this aggression at this stage of development and is what makes the form of swallowing salient. Furthermore, as I showed above, the father imago receives this projection because it is tied to social reality functions and must be protected. The anxiety related to the imago/father-substitute is the same aggression used against the parental imago by the egoistic, who, ultimately, can never defeat him without his return in defensive operations.

There is one further point in regard to the status of social reality for the father imago. The father imago, as the possessor of the mother, has as its prerogative the power that the ego renounces in the internalisation of the difference between the generations. In this case it means that the father imago enforces the demands of Time but remains outside of them himself. Therefore, he is generally given the representation of being "magical": the ability to fly; psychic powers, or powers outside of what normal people possess. As mentioned, the swallowing anxiety is related to the child's impulse to take the power of the father imago—the father-substitute's prized power is "assimilated by eating" as shown in the magic thinking of the cannibal (Freud, 1921, p. 105).

As mentioned above, I think it's important to be open to the idea of the different libidinal positions having different erotogenic zones and symbols in phantasy. The salience of the eye from the above mentioned "evil eye" is possibly a compliment to the cannibalistic incorporation. In Tausk (1933) the narcissistic stage is related to mimetic functions of the body that form the cognition of the ego at this stage. In pathology the body is felt to be controlled by a machine, power is drained away, thoughts are implanted or taken away, (etc.). However, Tausk has found the machine to be a "subsequent development" and that reference is first made to enemies, a lover, or a person (Tausk, 1933, p. 522). In an example he cites an example of the body being controlled from one of Freud's early cases; a patient felt that "her eyes were no longer properly placed in her head but entirely twisted out of position" and that "her lover was an evil, deceitful person who twisted eyes" (p. 525). Another patient felt that everyone she came across can read her thoughts and, as I'll get to soon, this is consistent with the general level of Being of the narcissistic stage (p. 536). The "third eye" is tied to psychic abilities, great hypnotists were said to put someone under trance with their gaze alone, and there are often patients who are unable to look the analyst in the eyes as if it's a form of conceit. It seems that while the egoistic fears losing his power, the intermixing of the two poles at this stage suggests that boundaries between self and other are established for the altruist. However, in full defusion her mind or body once again loses separation and comes under the power of the object.

In the later phallic level of Being the egoistic is measured against the father-substitutes who have posts or positions that confer Prestige and social hierarchy is included in this definition of power. In the narcissistic level of Being the egoistic is measured in his encounter with another person by witnessing, over time, the actual result of his acts, but there is no reference to social hierarchy as such. One can call the auto-erotic stage part-object because of the focus on the breast or phallus alone. However, the failure of the narcissistic stage castration complex to take actual objects (i.e., ego-interest and object-love remain wishes) doesn't sound like a full object either. Although, it must be granted that the narcissistic stage father imago seems to appear as a whole object. Freud, as mentioned above, seems to avoid these issues by making secondary narcissism and the observable distinction between ego and object drives in action, as opposed to wishes, the point of reference.

After introducing Tausk's influencing machine, as a "subsequent development", another idea is salient at this stage. We should be open to phases between the narcissistic oedipal and the social hierarchy I'll show at work in the anal oedipal stage. Anzieu (1987), for example, documents a skin-ego reference point and Winnicott (1953) mentions the development of a transitional object that likely go beyond the castration complexes being examined. The idea of the post-oedipal father complex stage being a development in every psychosexual phase will be discussed later on and could help make sense of these findings.

Although it isn't explicit like the aforementioned auto-erotic, narcissistic, and phallic stages, Freud's work suggests a stage between the narcissistic and the phallic in which social hierarchy first makes its appearance to demand perfection though enduring measurement. Freud does give a hint about when he believes this development of secondary narcissism begins. "Defaecation" he writes, "affords the first occasion on which the child must decide between a narcissistic [ego-interest] and an object-loving attitude (Freud, 1917c, p. 130). This means that the superego observably measures the ego's performance in relation to others and that striving, in both egoistic and altruistic ego drives and object drives, become observable. This observable measurement of the individual ego gives it a whole status and in reciprocity indicates a whole object.[5] Freud (1930) also gives us the example of a level of Being at this stage in his reference to "saints" who demonstrate "a universal love of mankind" (p. 102). In keeping with sublimation as rerouting the later phallic ego ideal to earlier stages he maintains "far-reaching mental changes … are necessary before this can happen[;] they [saintly people] protect themselves against the loss of the object by directing their love, not to single objects but to all men alike" (Freud, 1930, pp. 101–102). Without this sublimation, or in mere regression to the anal stage, Abraham notes that "good-heartedness … [as] incomplete object-love of this kind [means] a socially useful 'variety' [of person] is produced, which in essential respects is, nevertheless, inferior to full [phallic] object-love" (Abraham, 1923, p. 408). Additionally, the concept of the saint can also be further refined to a narcissistic stage sublimation in which the individual lives in solitude in a monastery or in nature and merely wishes love for people from afar.

Between the Time possessing narcissistic father imago with magical abilities and the Prestige possessing phallic father imago, I understand the anal father imago to possess the depersonalised quality of the Superlative. This means that as far as the subject egoistic has transference to someone that doesn't involve magical abilities but considers them as "the best", "the smartest", or "the most powerful" in relation to all other people ("all men alike"), it is his anal father transference. Even though the magic possessing narcissistic stage father is beyond Time and has a strong claim to the concept of "omnipotence" or "omniscience" these words are often associated with the anal father imago as well. The bridge, as I'll get to soon, is that a king was often seen as, or coming from, the divine. However, because the anal father imago rules over all people there is a direct sense of power; it is built into the relation of the father to "all people". In contrast, the narcissistic father possesses a transference that isn't located in social hierarchy and resembles a monster that lives outside of human communities or a helpful wizard who hides his magic from ordinary people. These instantiations depend on one's libidinal position and whether the father appears in his good or bad aspect.

In the literature the "omnipotent anal father" is something many analysts have brought up but which still has managed to defy formalisation in psychoanalytic thought. Ernest Jones (1951) in an early article writes of a perfect and omnipotent father imago that can be behind the concept of God. Chasseguet-Smirgel links oedipal regression to an omnipotent, indestructible imago of the anal stage and Melanie Klein writes of the "omnipotence of excrements" in displacements of power from imago to things (Chasseguet-Smirgel, 1974, pp. 355–356; Klein, 1932, p. 239, 280, 363). Kohut (1971) notes the archaic need for "limitless achievement and limitless acclaim" which seems like a definition of the superlative (p. 151). Additionally, striving not just for success but for absolute power is a very important to Individual Psychology. Adler (1946) writes that it

> introduces into our life a hostile and fighting tendency, robs us of the simplicity of our feeling and is always the cause of an estrangement from reality since it puts near to our hearts the idea

of attempting to over-power reality. Whoever takes this goal of godlikeness seriously or literally, will soon be compelled to flee from real life and compromise, by seeking a life within life; if fortunate in art, but more generally in pietism, neurosis, or crime. (Adler, 1946, p. 8)

Adler lacked an interest in psychosexual development and only referenced a single "drive" or "will to power" so the differentiation between the phallic and the anal phallus isn't part of his theory. In contrast, Annie Reich (1960) is able to provide the symbolic representation of the anal level of Being when she studies the phantasy of patients competing with all others to possess a single phallus. She writes:

> in a number of cases I have found the fantasy that only one grandiose phallus exists in the whole world. When the patient is in possession of it or is identified with it, everyone else is deprived of it and thus totally destroyed. In the negative phase, the tables are turned: the grandiose phallus belongs to somebody else—perhaps to its rightful, original owner—who, full of contempt, now destroys the patient. Either way, the acquisition of this glorified organ is accomplished through violent aggression ... the still completely sexualized and glorified object is set up as a primitive ego ideal, as something he longs to be ... (A. Reich, 1960, pp. 225–226)

This single anal phallus stands in contrast to the many possible skills or fields of knowledge that one can compete in at the phallic stage. To support this connection, in our common language we often use shit to reference the superlative. To "kick the shit out of someone" is to give a superlative beating, to be an ass-kisser or brown noser is to be the most servile or to want to be loved the most, being the most beautiful is contrast by looking like shit, and so on. Grunberger in his study of anal object relations finds they consist of a "hierarchy including the principle of absolute domination, personified by a God or a 'charismatic chief'" (Grunberger, 1977, p. 109). With this in mind, a king who ruled a nation was taken to be of divine origin and many artists or geniuses were thought to be godlike or divinely inspired. In this way I've come to understand that while the father-substitutes at the phallic stage have to do with one's status reputation for success within one's community that is measured by wealth, academic degrees, or membership to exclusive groups, at the anal stage father-substitutes appear as the people who are the "pillars of society" or civilisation. Kings, Presidents, popes, scientific and artistic geniuses, etc. whose power is superlative or the closest to godlike (omnipotent) or those whose paradigms of thought are the basis of civilisation and are the closest to omniscient are the anal fathers.[6] However, there is the sense, that once we leave the current state of civilisation and ask who is the most powerful or important person who ever lived, that we enter into the narcissistic level of Being. To make a big enough contribution to civilisation, and therefore to history, seems to grant an immortality that references Time and creates the individual as a singularity. Following this line of thought, the quotes from A. Reich and some others above seem more appropriate for the narcissistic phallus, but it is difficult to say since they didn't pursue their investigation from the side of phenomenology, or didn't reference a social ontology if they did. The matching of relevant erotogenic zones and part-objects with a level of Being will be key in helping to clear up confusion in such cases.

The "double tie" of putting the father-substitute in one's ego ideal exists here and is contrasted with the anal castration complex. This provides the ontological choice of competing to be the Superlative, or being a human being who accepts "society" or the hegemonic systems of power or knowledge. The anal castration complex is seen in those who compulsively work on their intellectual or physical pursuits towards the goal of the superlative. The academic or artist who is trying to invent a new paradigm of thought that will "change everything" or the "soldier" or "fighter" who is working his way towards being "the toughest" or those who live for the applause and worship from crowds or groups of people. In contrast to the phallic father imago in which the would-be academic may challenge the superiority of his professor or his advisor, at the anal level he may challenge the institution of the university as such and hold that he is after a purer knowledge that isn't found there. This sense of some place of power behind officialised institutional power often shows up in paranoiac constructions of aliens, the illuminati, a secret stage agency, etc. that threatens one. J. Bernstein (1975–1976) gives a very valuable character study on what he calls the autistic character in which the lonely ivory tower pursuit of perfection is linked to the phase appropriate cognitive style of deduction (p. 542). However, it is outside of my focus to examine the different phase-specific perceptual-consciousness systems of the ego, save the examination of phallic semiotics in the appendix.

The castration anxiety and the impulse towards the father-substitute is to kill or cause death. As mentioned above, this isn't from an internal knowledge of death, which can't be known any more than perfection can by the finite mind. If the auto-erotic stage has a "body-ego" in which body and mind have a functional unity, and the phallic stage has an "image-ego", then there is something of a "spirit-ego" at the anal stage.[7] I take this from the expression that a person can be have "a lot of spirit", which can refer to the will. Early aggressive impulses can be differentiated from the later phallic stage aggressive impulses by examining the concept of sadim. Sadism, in the strict sense, is aimed at inflicting pain on another and requires a theory of mind to enjoy the other's suffering. Freud recognises that "the infliction of pain plays no part among the original purposive actions of the instinct" and that in early stages of development the "child takes no account of whether or not he inflicts pains, nor does he intend to do so" (Freud, 1915, p. 128). It is only with the creation of the image-ego in which suffering in relation to one's fallen reputation or social humiliation is experienced that knowledge of the object's mind can safely be said to exist. In this case we use "sadism" in the sense of attacking another person's reputation or self-esteem. Before this the term destructive impulses and their relation to an object's body and not an object's mind is in order. Early analysts such as Van Ophuijsen (1929) write of physically destructive impulses aimed at the bodies of others that is distinct from the later developments of sadism, a vendetta, etc. that relate to the "image-ego" but can "unite with [these] other tendencies" (Van Ophuijsen, pp. 140–141). The anal castration anxiety seems to be the mid point in which the object's psyche is attributed with power in relation to, or above, all other people, and an existence that can be negated in death with the individual experiencing some pleasure in this end.[8]

In Chapter Two I argued that the phallic-oedipal conscience deals with aggressive impulses concerning the image or reputation of others. At this level of development there is an "image-ego" that is driven to success and social sadism to want to humiliate, revenge oneself upon, or ruin the reputation of others. These impulses along with cheating, or using others as stepping stones to get ahead are inhibited by a conscience of fairness. In the conclusion I indicated that the relation to the physically destructive mob in which the individual externalises his conscience onto the group leader is actually an earlier manifestation of group psychology. Instead, politics and externalising one's conscience of fairness onto ideologues, opinion-leaders, and other phallic-fathers with status better characterises the phallic-oedipal. In regard to the anal mob there is an interesting Janus-faced quality in that sublimation can reroute the phallic ego ideal to the ideal of striving for the phallus so that one will be the pillar of society in regard to one's skill, knowledge, or place of power but, at the same time, in the presence of a group of people the old form of cognition seems to recall the feeling of these high stakes. In working with substance abuse groups I've often got the impression that narcissistic individuals, beyond the feelings of their self-importance can't resist competition for control in this situation.

Along with the omnipotence of wishes in the narcissistic stage, the lack of social hierarchy there also suggests possible sublimations regarding the ego ideal. Self-reliance and living like one is something different than other humans, is a recurring ideal for some patients. To be clear, if it's merely a reaction to paranoid phantasies then it isn't sublimation or an ideal. Interestingly, this stoic way of life is also often in evidence without an explicit value system of stoicism or a similar world view. Additionally, as mentioned above, not just being at the top of the social pyramid but being the best there's ever been, similarly establishes a subject egoistic as a singularity.

On the altruistic pole a similar parallel between the anal and narcissistic ego ideal is visible. I've had patients who felt the imperative to devote their lives to the service of others and the ideal of transforming the school system, prison system, and basic institutions into something that nurtures and helps humankind. Above, I contrasted these "saintly" types with conception of the saint who wishes others well without actually living among them or helping them. Again, to reroute to the narcissistic ego ideal in sublimation is to move beyond measuring oneself against the others and in Nietzsche (1982) we again find a penetrating view of this in his psychological assessment of the "redeemer type":

> this "bringer of glad tidings" died as he had lived, as he had taught—not to "redeem men" but to show how one must live. This practice is his legacy to man-kind: his behavior before the judges, before the catch-poles, before the accusers and all kinds of slander and scorn—his behavior on the cross. He does not resist, he does

not defend his right, he takes no step which might ward off the worst; on the contrary, he provokes it. And be begs, he suffers, he loves with those, in those, who do him evil. Not to resist, not to be angry, not to hold responsible—but to resist not even the evil one—to love him. (Nietzsche, 1982, pp. 608–609)

Interestingly, Nietzsche's description of the altruist who offers no resistance to others, but still manages to provoke their ire, points to a binary with the description of the egoistic. The former behaves, in some sense, like his needs shouldn't exist, while the latter behaves like his needs are the only ones that should exist. The "double tie" of this ego ideal does seem applicable to group psychology in that certain people want to cause awe or wonder in others or can feel like an abomination, monstrous, or something greater or less than human before them. This can sometimes reference Time, such as when a person regards himself as human but "from the future/past" but, feeling like one is part divine, alien, a vampire, etc., in both good and bad ways, has shown up in my patients. Moreover, just as inferiority would possess a different quality based upon the form of perfection that one is striving for, so that the opportunity for shame in the subject egoist's impotence deepens in earlier levels of Being, the same could be expected for the subject altruist. Nietzsche sees that this feeling of conceit can reach the level where resisting someone else's desire, to assert oneself as a separate individual is felt as wrong.

In contrast to the sublimation in Nietzsche's sketch, I've encountered many patients whose lives are largely governed by their inability to say no to others and therefore they schedule their lives around avoiding contact with certain people so they don't have to turn them down or come up with excuses. At later stages, speaking in a group or asking others to give one some time or assistance can be felt as conceit, while later, receiving compliments and admiration feels inappropriate and unseemly. The shame of ingratitude and assuming the father's prerogatives threaten the subject altruist just as failing to be recognised as the father's equal is the subject egoist's shame.

VI

As I indicated last chapter, the imago is the reference for the superego's guilt prohibition until the latency superego. At the phallic stage the guilt conscience can be externalised back onto a phallic father-substitute so that fairness in work groups is disregarded and personal success is extolled in political values. I also indicated that the relation to the mob indicates an archaic conscience there that operates in a similar way. In recognising earlier physically destructive impulses such as killing, robbing, etc. that differ from sadism proper, externalisation of the conscience regarding these destructive acts onto a mob leader, suggests an anal superego. Ferenzci (1925) has famously coined sphincter morality (p. 379), Klein (1928) notes anal phantasies of robbing the body of another tied to reparations (pp. 256–257), and Erik Erikson (1963) links the anal stage to "the principle of law and order" (p. 254). The anal superego is not an intellectual idea about how one's actions are destructive or harmful to the body of another but instead, the subjective feelings that are paired with physically destructive impulses are connected to the prohibition from a father imago who reserves the right alone to these acts. The institution of the law or the police are the depersonalised anal version of "social anxiety" in which destructive acts and robbing may be kept at bay from shame of being regarded as a criminal. In the same way, social anxiety that references feeling abject or monstrous for cannibalistic or other impulses denotes narcissistic stage ontology.

While aggression towards paternal and maternal substitutes is prohibited at the Oedipus complex and retained in defusion, or the subsequent castration complex, conscience in relation to siblings or those of one's generation is established in the following father complex. Several analysts note that throughout development there is a stage of full identification that may not be reached and leaves one more susceptible to pathology. For example Hendrick (1936) examines this as partial vs. full identification (p. 338); Klein (1940) as establishing, or not, the "internal good object" (p. 153); and Kohut (1971) identifies it as transmuting internalisation (pp. 74, 82, 100). The failure to form self-observations that possess equality with others and ego ideals that are thereby reduced in the perfection they demand means that such an individual is under much more pressure than others. However, economically, this also means such an individual has more energy to spend in the striving for his oedipal ideal.

The urethral stage is a likely candidate for the father complex at the anal phase of development. Indeed, some early analysts have pointed to the confusion between the two. For example Coriot (1924) writes that the urethal character "has many features allied to, in fact, almost identical with, the anal-erotic character as first pointed out by Freud"

(Coriat, 1924, p. 430). It is this conscience, which some might not even perform the instinctual renunciation to form, that is externalised upon the anal father as mob leader or the general in war that allows for killing. Additionally, although the anal castration complex prohibition concerns the father-substitute only, in eros or fusion with him it is likely that a feeling of wanting to extend this prohibition to others is in operation for the subject egoistic. As hinted above, the father complex, or post-oedipal stage, should also complicate the levels of Being that I've formulated, but this investigation will have to wait for another work.

VII

As part of the ego ideal and the motivational system of humanity, these different levels of social ontology aren't hidden. Towards this end I'd like to submit that in the standard Sci Fi or Fantasy epic film series, like *Star Wars, Lord of the Rings, Highlander, The Matrix* etc. that these levels of Being, are in plain sight. In *Star Wars* (1977, 1980, 1983), for example, Darth Vader plays the role of the phallic father in his bad aspect. He has a place of authority as commander of the troops and is depicted as possessing superior skill in combat and in operation of a spaceship. The anal father is represented by the Emperor, who is the ruler of the galaxy and is Darth Vader's supraordinate. "The force" is a magical power that allows people to control things with their minds and works in confluence with the imagos of other stages. Yoda, for example, lives solitarily outside of social hierarchies and would be a narcissistic father-substitute, in its good aspect, as is the ghost of Obi Wan. Additionally, the fact that *Star Wars* takes space as its setting and creates new rival worlds to our own is an example of the defusion at the auto-erotic level. The "death star" that annihilates planets is itself obliterated showing maximal sadism as discussed above in regard to Space.

In the *Lord of the Rings* (2001, 2002, 2003) there is competition for the single ring that controls all other rings and would place one in the Superlative position "to rule them all". The ring also associates quite readily to a finger which is a nice phallic symbol. Additionally, the solitary magicians in *LOTR* and the magic that the ring bestows also indicates the narcissistic stage importance there as well. The film also illustrates the creation of new worlds and new life forms and in an important scene at the end of the first (2001) and reprised in the second movie (2002), Gandolf falls with a great demon and this fall, becomes elaborated as a trip through the universe from which he returns as the white wizard. Frodo's mission to save humankind and the tension of his struggle with conceit and choosing his own happiness instead of this mission is the major arc. Frodo's relationship to the ring is strongly contrasted to the desires of egoistic characters who would like to take the ring in order to rule the world. Gollum's character also illustrates that the ring needn't be used for the end of ruling everyone or to dominate others. Moreover, Gollum's happiness in being alone with the ring suggests that it can also act as a transitional object of the narcissistic stage. Another protagonist, Aragon, struggles to accept his lineage and the need for him to be assertive and lead. Considering his love interest in Arwen, an elven woman, when he was raised by elves himself (i.e., she could be seen as a sister), the phallic father complex seems to be relevant for his character.

In *Highlander* (1986) and *The Matrix* (1999) the narcissistic stage is prominent. In *Highlander* immortals fight under the imperative that "there can be only one" and there isn't a reference to social hierarchy or ruling over the human family. After one immortal kills another his power is assimilated. This, along with the depiction of immortals being able to feel each other's presence displays the narcissistic stage level of Being of encountering another non-human who threatens to "swallow" one. However, the duels, which are based upon who is the most skilled with their weapon, show a confluence with the phallic castration complex. In the final showdown with the main villain, who has kidnapped MacLeod's love interest, the phallic castration complex comes into prominence.[9] In *The Matrix* a similar level of Being is present with computer agents taking over the bodies of people around the heroes and attacking them with superhuman strength and celerity. An anal level of Being is present with the idea of machines ruling and oppressing humankind and the hero, Neo, being a messianic figure prophesied to altruistically save human civilisation. Compared to the auto-erotic defusion in *Star Wars* and *Lord of the Rings*, in which phantasy worlds and the relevant castration anxiety are fully in evidence, an auto-erotic father complex is suggested in the dualism between the illusory matrix humans live in and the dystopian rule of the machines in the actual world. The choice to stay in the matrix illusion *vs.* struggle in the real world is embodied in the character Cypher who betrays Neo and the rebels.

I haven't attempted to be exhaustive in my analysis of these films. However, their popularity means that most readers will have seen them and therefore get a general sense for Freud's social ontology in action. In my experience, phantasies of a social (ego drive) nature that reference the patient in regard to "all humankind", being the only one who should exist, their reputation in the community, etc., are just as salient as erotogenic zones in analysis. Ultimately, if analysts can find a common theoretical language, I think that the real work of finding what clinical technique works best for a certain type of patient can begin. There will never be step by step or "cook-book" instructions for an analysis but between the patient being wholly unique and dogmatic assertions of depth structures, there is a middle ground of common language that references motivations across these levels of Being and across psychic bisexuality.

VIII

In summary, the general sketch I have provided of the different levels of Being is also given a trans-historical representation by the fathers of Greek mythology. Uranus, as the representation of the sky opens up the dimension of Space upon the earth (Gaia). Cronos, the God of Time, is the supreme power in the world and swallows all of his children, save for Zeus, who, as we know takes power from him to become king of all the Gods and the Superlative power in a hierarchy of other Gods. Then, on top of this Superlative relation we have a blending of second generation Gods into mortal heroes that show the important theme of hubris for one's talents (for example, Arachne, Bellerophon) and deal with aggression towards parents or authority (for example, Oedipus, Elektra). I don't think that the ancients somehow understood social ontology without the benefit of the work of modern philosophy and psychoanalysis. Rather, the need for pictoral forms (or "picture-thinking") shows that whatever insights into repetitions that the ancients possessed, they didn't recognise the social ontological underpinning of the drive.

Coming to the formulation of competition for power from Perfection and restoration of belonging from Death, as a modification of the eternal conflict Freud saw between Eros and the death drive, has made me appreciate the grand scope with which he approached his subject. In another grand formulation concerning the unconscious, I think Freud also finds a way to come to the assistance of Kleinians. Although Klein's work has often been criticised for its adultomorphism I hope I have shown both that there are larger ontological issues that provide reference points, along with the salient part-objects and erotogenic zones, that take the emphasis off of the child's cognition. Additionally, the status of the father, or his phallus, as a symbol of the not-mother that comes into synthesis in the social body, means that the child doesn't have to be observing complicated relationships early on and that relations to the mother, or primary caregiver, alone can provide the stimulus for much of the earliest development. The child's immature cognition at these early stages is used as an argument against its ability to repress or store memories. However, once psychoanalysis is linked to ontology the place of repression is no longer in the individual's mind but in the space in between the self and other.

I've followed Klein in suggesting that psychosexual development is the slow intermixing of the egoistic and altruistic poles and in contrast to this development or "becoming" of the child, it is possible that there is a negative or "not-becoming" state. This not-becoming state, again, is part of our social nature and not a function of the mind of an atomistic being. Freud (1920) hypothesises this as the "timeless unconscious" and compares it to Kant's designation of the noumenal:

> at this point I shall venture to touch for a moment upon a subject which would merit the most exhaustive treatment. As a result of certain psycho-analytic discoveries, we are to-day in a position to embark on a discussion of the Kantian theorem that time and space are "necessary forms of thought." We have learnt that unconscious mental processes are in themselves "timeless." This means in the first place that they are not ordered temporally, that time does not change them in any way and that the idea of time cannot be applied to them. *These are negative characteristics which can only be clearly understood if a comparison is made with conscious mental processes* ... This mode of functioning may perhaps constitute another way of providing a shield against stimuli. I know that these remarks must sound very obscure, but I must limit myself to these hints. (Freud, 1920, p. 28, emphasis mine)

Outside of the subjective sense of Space and Time isn't a noumenal self who is a rational chooser, but rather something that must be based upon our primary relatedness. In this place of not-becoming what becomes traumatic and over-stimulates the conscious mind, in its becoming, persists as a shadow. When an individual turns away from fusion with the father's social body or social reality these shadows can come to life and may loom so long that he or she no longer ventures into daylight.

Working with these grand concepts I'm aware that Freud's work in pathology may only be recapitulating just a small portion of what Hegel (1977) has already pointed to in his inversion of metaphysics. However, where Hegel's rationalism may have possibly taken him astray, Freud's empiricism may provide more concrete coordinates for the work of examining transcendental idealism and the depersonalisation of parental imagos. Along with Hegel, Pierce and other developmental thinkers in semiotics, the research of child psychologists will, no doubt, also be very important. However, for anyone who can share my enthusiasm for this vision, a problem remains. For the post-Hegelian imperative found in Nietzsche and Marx—to not merely understand the world but to change it—appears in Freud's work. How can one be content with merely citing psychoanalysts in attempts to prove one's superior knowledge without showing one's understanding through clinical success?

Notes

1. The Lacanian formulation of the "desire of the mother" for the child to strive to possess a certain signifier and the "wished for self-image" of the ego psychologists apply here as suggested in Chapter Two (Fink, 1995, pp. 54–55; Milrod, 2002, p. 134). However, other analysts' work, such as McDougall (1974), suggests that seduction by the mother and the adoption of her "phallic image" is a non-universal stage in development.

2. Freud relates primal repression as "fixation[:] ... one instinct or instinctual component fails to accompany the rest along the anticipated normal development path ... then behaves in relation to the system of the unconscious, like one that is repressed" (Freud, 1911b, p. 67).

3. I do feel inclined to soften this last judgement. Where "understanding" words is concerned, the infant would be required to prove this power through his or her use of them. However, everyone is familiar with "baby-talk" and the use of words not to signify but in delight of their sensuous quality. It may well be that on the passive-altruistic side that words in their sensuousness could be a "transitional object" of

sorts for the child's desire for closeness to the caregiver. Klein (1932), in fact, has linked problems with learning languages and hatred toward foreign languages (for their dissonance compared to the cadences and tones of one's language, no doubt) to very early stages of development (pp. 241–243). At the end of this article I indicate that relation between the Oedipus complex and father complex at the phallic stage likely exists at earlier stages and that this would add further levels of Being, or modfications, to the ones offered here.

4. I'd also like to complicate the simple picture of the claim that the narcissistic (stage) father imago is linked to "swallowing" castration anxiety by adding the story of the Three Little Pigs. In this story the first anxiety situation is the wolf "huffing and puffing" on the houses before the second anxiety situation of being eaten would occur. Elkin (1972) holds that the "primordial Other ... in dreams is most directly symbolized by the all-encompassing, immaterial, and spontaneously animated air or wind (pp. 398–9). Similarly, in the Odyssey, Odysseus leaves the man-eating cyclops to experience disappointment from Aeolus' winds when they had almost got him home. Thus, to account for these two behaviours of the father we must, as Fairbairn points out, recognise that the "father is treated at first in the same way as mother and his figure is combined with hers by layering and by fusion" (Padel, 1991, p. 602). There are other analysts who also recognise the transcription of the relations of the mother to the father, including Ruth Mack Brunswick (1940) whose work Freud oversaw, but it is outside of the scope of my investigation here. A detailed study will be needed to determine what is universal and what is a non-universal adaptation. Additionally, in my clinical experience, the house or home in the Three Little Pigs story has significance as a parental imago and has appeared as a manifest figure of triangulation with some psychotic patients. One woman wanted to move into the "beautiful house" of a friend and her daughter was attributed with the motivation to move in just to "snatch" it from her. Many other patients only feel safe in their home and the rest of the outside world is dangerous and unpredictable for them.

5. Abraham (1923) sees the anal drives as having an "incomplete object" *vs.* the "full object" attained in the genital or father complex (after the phallic Oedipus complex) but both would still be regarded as whole (p. 408).

6. A child or naïve youth might also have an anal father transference for people who don't even have these ties to the institutions of power. Anyone who confronts them as a phallic father might also receive the anal transference with the phallic one. Then, as the individual takes on more of the knowledge or skills of civilisation the local senator, wealthy

business owner of the community, or ivy league educated professor who have ties to superlative institutions might receive the transference.

7. The designation of the ego for the narcissistic stage seems to best be called a "soul-ego". This is based upon the expressions that someone can be a soul man, bare one's soul (inner most thoughts), be a lost soul (have no direction), or love someone with all one's heart and soul. However, I'm wary of using the designation because of the mystical implication some might draw from it.

8. Additionally, death can be located in the body itself as hypochondria demonstrates and Klein directly links it to phantasies of faeces in the body and introjection of the hated father (Klein, 1932, p. 206; 1958, p. 88).

9. Even though the anal castration complex rivalry to rule the human family isn't depicted overtly, it is possible that it is still captured in the image of the much greater size and sword of the villain.

CONCLUSION

In this book I have investigated Freud's Copernican revolution of the drive to establish psychic bisexuality, social ontology in the superego, and the centrality of the Oedipus complex. Psychic bisexuality provides a horizontal axis through which one asks if the person in question seeks power and admiration for their skills, knowledge, beauty, values, or judgement or whether he or she seeks belonging and approval for their hard work, self-sacrifice, their goodness, being interesting, or their style. Social ontology provides a vertical axis though which one asks if the person in question is working around issues involving Prestige and their reputation in the community, the Superlative and a place among the greats or a place among the lowly, Time and the magic that escapes it and a place where one is alone, and Space where life exists in another world. The Oedipus complex in the child's development is identification with the father as possessing the mother and the acceptance of this imago and the father-substitutes one takes into the ego ideal. Afterwards, it references the shame of the father-substitute or the self in the lack of integrity that sees the individual choose to defuse. The eros with the father becomes phobos or fear of fusion. The respect for the other becomes respect for the self, and the loyalty to one's own autnomous desires becomes loyalty to the other. The incest barrier is breached and one seeks to possess or restore the phallus with the imperative that one must match the father and the concomitant tensions of not filling his shoes, filling them, or deceiving oneself or others that one doesn't care about shoes.

An in-depth examination of a historical culture would take us too far ashore, but even without the study of particular cultures it is possible to lay the debate of the universality of the Oedipus complex to rest. In the way Freud defined it, the Oedipus complex exists in any culture that recognises the difference between neophytes and elders who are accorded respect for more skill and knowledge (even if the knowledge is based on magic instead of empiricism). None of the neo-Freudians dispute the recognition of the universality of the difference between the generations in culture or the religion, marriage, morality of the subsequent father complex. Rather, the problem is a termino-logical one in that the castration complex is the term that references the defusion from the oedipal father imago or the pathological form of the Oedipus complex. While the difference between the generations requires that the Oedipus complex has been traversed and the phallic father imago has been established, the social conditions that lead to defusion, retribution from father-substitutes, or failure to form the guilt conscience, aren't necessarily trans-historical and the neo-Freudians have a very strong point to make here (Reich, 1972, p. 170). For exam-ple, Reich (1972) points to the large difference between early cultures in regard to mental illness and the treatment of women (pp. 127–128, pp. 156–157).

Recognising the lack of knowledge of paternity in early political-economies and that God (and the devil) figure so prominently in psycho-sis, the father as procreator must arise from the idea of God and not the other way around. The male sex, as the not-mother, comes to symbolise God *qua* procreator, who created and possesses the mother. As noted by Reich (1972) the maternal uncle is the earlier, earthly counterpart who is the head of the family in one matriarchal society. When the biological father is understood to be the procreator and head of the family then strife in the personal relationship between husband and wife can poten-tially effect the phallic father imago. Unhappiness in the marriage can colour how the children see authority figures in general, where before, the maternal uncle was distant enough from the mother that his author-ity wouldn't be contested.[1] This subject is very complicated and will require its own future investigation. I only wish to indicate that I'm aware of the inconsistency of using the term father-substitute when the father isn't known at first.

I have attempted to be sensitive in my formulations to the important input that Marxian sociology must provide, although I barely hinted at this. Only when civilisation includes a certain amount of technology does the connection between seed and plant and father and child arise. This in turn allows a connection to the father that didn't exist before to arise and sets into motion mass defusion at the phallic oedipal. Technology increases and the ability of one group to enslave others and keep the ruler at a distance from the ruled likely sets into motion mass defusion at the anal oedipal. Having a ruler who is taboo, and with whom the people don't interact, allows for a more idealised (anal) transference to occur which wouldn't happen when a leader was known personally in the community. This process continues on because the technological creations of humankind allow certain classes to gain ascendency and silently reorganise social interactions.

This insight is implied in the sociologically informed writings of Abram Kardiner where he raises the important question of whether anal character traits, for example, are present from the beginning or arise from the influence of civilisation (Kardiner, 1939, pp. 391–393). Kardiner makes a compelling argument that sociology plays a more significant role than Freud recognised in creating pre-oedipal character that I won't examine here. However, even though certain pre-oedipal character traits might not exist in primitive political-economies, Kardiner does recognise basic phallic-egoistic traits like jealousy to be universal. Therefore, even though some post-modernists may contend that there are examples of cultures in which polyandry, for example, is the practice and that this proves that jealousy is a socially produced trait, and not part of any trans-historical active-phallic ego drives, they would do better to look beneath the surface of the practices. Kardiner (1939) writes

> no society can impose upon the individual that he should either feel or not feel jealousy; society can only curb its manifestations, render its usefulness for adaptation minimal, or devise methods for restoring the state of equilibrium in the individual. A society may, however, render the manifestations of jealousy overt and even encourage its manifestations ... It may be pointed out that the Todas are a people among whom there is no jealousy have a

> polyandrous system of marriage. ... however [in their religion] there is a special place in the netherworld for those who feel jealousy, thereby clearly indicating that there are sanctions against the manifestation of jealousy ... (Kardiner, 1939, p. 466)

There is clearly a dialectic between individual character or "psychic constitution" and the social ideals of the father complex and latency and I'd like to refer any reader who thinks that discourse alone shapes the individual to the appendix. I don't have anything to add to Kardiner's thought here, but recognising the dialectic involved also makes the nature *vs.* nurture debate salient and I'd like to add a quick note about that. In Freud's model, psychic constitution is something that is both heritable and malleable though child-rearing practices as noted in the concept of the "'complemental series'" (Freud, 1917b, pp. 346–347; 1939, p. 73). Freud overcomes the binary of nature and nurture by indicating that the third term of the traumatic/adaptation and its repetition is the key factor. For example, one identical twin may become schizophrenic while the other doesn't and the inherited disposition may have been contained by the caregivers without becoming a trauma in the latter case. Similarly, a person with no schizophrenia in the family may experience bad parenting that leads to an individual reaction that becomes traumatic and suffer a psychosis later in life.

Both Marx and Freud argue that the materialism comes first in either the form of technology or in the id drives and their projects are inseparably linked. The technology that influences social organisation, for example, didn't arise from an observable link between seeds and plants that someone noticed and brought to the group with the rational idea that it was better to plant food than gather it all day. Rather, as Roheim (1941) points out, these things are based upon unconscious phantasy that later was given an instrumental use:

> it shows very little insight into the mental processes of primitive man to believe that he is likely to plant yams because he has come to the conclusion that they will bring him a plentiful crop in the future, or that he keeps dogs because they are useful in hunting kangaroos. The carefree children of the jungle or desert never think of the morrow in pre-agricultural societies. But if they have associated phantasies of destroying the body with taking the yams out of Mother Earth, it would be easy to see how the reparation

aspect of those phantasies might lead to a replanting, that this in turn might lead to an observation of the crop, and so secondarily to a practical result from the endopsychically conditioned activity. Or, if man extended the mother–child situation to the puppy of the wild dog, these dogs, brought up in human society, might prove useful in the chase; but this was a result of a play activity which nobody could have foreseen. My view, therefore, is that the bulk of human culture, even in its adaptational or ego-aspects, arises out of play or ritual activities. The reason for these activities lies in the infantile situation, and they acquire survival value secondarily by assimilating a part of the environment to man's needs. This is the way of culture—the transformation of id into ego. (Roheim, 1941, pp. 162–163)

Roheim isn't saying that people from primitive political-economies lack intelligence but just that the area it is applied to is much smaller, and that the technology that does arises isn't from a scientific stance. Since humans are social animals who are primarily related, the earlier political-economies require much more participation and it's an ideological error in judgement to see its members actively observing the environment for rational maximising of time and energy. Moreover, evidence suggests that the hunters and gatherers didn't simply democratically decide to change their way of life to agriculture in the Neolithic revolution based upon the utility of farming once its practice became salient. In Cohen and Armelagos' *Paleopathology at the Origins of Agriculture* (1984) we find that diseases caused by mineral and vitamin deficiency (i.e., rickets and scurvy) were common among farmers but virtually unknown among hunter-gatherers (pp. 68–69). Importantly, Cohen notes "conspicuous health differences ... between Kings and commoners", which leads to the conclusion that the only rational maximising where health was concerned was restricted to the upper class (ibid., p. 73).

Both psychoanalysis and Marxism have unsavory insights into human beings and their social organisations that challenge the egoist's need for control and the altruist's need to see goodness in others. Psychoanalysis needs altruists who will let phenomenology and their sense of different types be their guide, and not dogmatists who want to hang on to the fame of the founder of a school or claim their technique is the only way to practice. Marxism needs egoists who want merit to determine social organisation and not the rich passing on their wealth to their children who will pass it on to speculators and advertisers. The two joining together, along with the equality of men and women being fully established, suggests the cultural attainment of the father-complex. This follows Freud's progression from animism, to religion, and a nascent science that corresponds to the phallic-oedipal (Freud, 1913, p. 88).

I'd like to give my last word to the altruists who have begun to enter the profession in higher and higher numbers. Freud was an empiricist and often chided the philosophical system-making types who would, in procrustean fashion, deny or bend the facts so that their theories would be correct. However, psychoanalysis has splintered into many different schools and seen many former analysts start their own form of psychology. In this state of pluralism, many people no longer seek to perform a synthesis but rather to enshrine pluralism as a basic postulate of subjective existence. However, these people often attack the objective sciences and like Sinis, another bandit Theseus faced, these people can't accept that a theory can describe some aspect of reality. They can only tolerate the notion that we can see reality in separate and unique parts that can't be connected. The functional mindset is: we can have glimpses of God's grace but never know anything definitive about Him, nor anything definitive about ourselves, as His creation. God may grant us a moment of inspiration in some psychological theory, but it is hubris to turn this inspiration into something true about the mind. I understand their distrust of theory and I hope I have been able to stick to common language enough for others to resonate with the depth structures of perfection and death. I'd like to end with a quotation from Plato:

> ... but first there is a certain experience we must be careful to avoid ... That we must not become misologues, as people become misanthropes. There is no greater evil one can suffer than to hate reasonable discourse. Misology and misanthropy arise in the same way. Misanthropy comes when a man without knowledge or skill has placed great trust in someone and believes him to be altogether truthful, sound and trustworthy; then, a short time afterwards he finds him to be wicked and unreliable, and then this happens in another case; when one has frequently had that experience, especially with those whom one believed to be one's closest

friends, then, in the end, after many blows, one comes to hate all men and to believe that no one is sound in any way at all … This is a shameful state of affairs … and obviously due to an attempt to have human relations without any skill in human affairs.—Plato, *Phaedo*.

Note

1. In the example of the Trobriand Islanders, Malinowski (1922) holds that many of the males have a "characteristic ambition, vanity and desire to be renowned and well spoken of" (ibid., 118). This indicates a defusion from the father-imago has occurred. However, the castration complex, in this case, doesn't lead to mental illness because there are social sanctions against the father-substitutes seeking revenge. The son needn't fear retribution nor have to repress overwhelming aggression: "[i]n various parts of the world there are societies in which a sister's son teases and otherwise behaves disrespectfully towards his mother's brother. In these instances the joking relationship seems generally to be asymmetrical. For example the nephew may take his uncle's property but not vice-versa; or, as amongst the Nama Hottentos, the nephew may take a fine beast from his uncle's herd and the uncle in return takes a wretched beast from that of the nephew"(McGee, 2003, p. 184).

On Wittgenstein's private language argument

In this appendix I will present the private language argument of Wittgenstein in order to show the nature of the sign (signifier + signified) and how his account provides a foundation for the common language phenomenological approach I've taken in this book. Wittgenstein, like Freud, gives examples and arguments for his position and I will share these in order to defend my approach against potential criticism from post-modernists, relativists, and the views of some post-structuralists. I don't examine any specific criticism and acknowledge that to some degree I'm setting up a straw man for positions that are often more nuanced. However, my experience in sharing some of my work is that my reader doesn't share his or her own criticism or apprehensions but instead asks how I'd deal with the criticism of a straw man's position. This appendix is for their concerns.

Through Wittgenstein's private language argument I'll argue that the existence of words for different motivations, emotions, and sensations can't arise from our own sensations or feelings of them. Therefore the fact that they exist is based upon the ability of those with EQ to judge the physical expressions, behaviours, and intentions of others in a way that is consistent enough to create agreement among a community, and therefore give these words "meaning". Not everyone possesses EQ and we recognise that there are people on the autistic spectrum that don't notice "social cues" like the other person's boredom in conversation with them. We also recognise that some people possess what is called "wisdom" and this comes from the person being able to predict the behaviour of others and rightly judge their motivations and feelings that the others can assent to. This doesn't necessarily have a connection to a person having studied psychology or any such subject in university. Rather, it is better to existentially judge that there are people in one's community who others go to for advice, who have a reputation for their "good sense", and demonstrate the ability to help others see past their repetitions or lower their character defences, by the avowal of the beneficiary.[1] For those who lack EQ, and claim that it cannot exist, this aspect of the private language argument hopefully directs them to the possibility that it isn't "feminine irrationalism" but their own inadequacy and defences against feeling that are at work. Lastly, there are also intellectual positions that seem to be based upon their adherents having good EQ but because of their defences, they also would like to deny that the judgement of motivations, emotions, and sensations can have a trans-historical existence. I will conclude the appendix by illustrating how the private language argument forces the hand of different intellectual positions based upon what Reich (1973b) has called mechanistic and mystical forms of thinking, to which I'll add relativistic thinking.

The philosophy of Kant famously left Western thought deadlocked at antinomies between the existence or non-existence of God, the freedom of the will or determinism, and so on, that still polarise debates to this day. His claims of the synthetic nature of mathematics, the schematism of sensibility and understanding, and the inscrutability of motivation represent the foundations for some of the antinomies and basis for the potential rational essence of mind and will. I will argue that these are errors that the lesser known philosophy of the late Wittgenstein has dispelled. Where Kant uses transcendental arguments that are based upon the work that the mind must do in order for the world and things in it to appear as they do "for me", Wittgenstein argues that our phenomenal perception isn't the heart of the issue. Instead, he offers transcendental arguments that concern the community of language-using beings. Moving the argument from the individual to the group level also places Wittgenstein into the semiotic shift of the twentieth century.

The existence of mathematics has long been a stronghold for the inherent rationality, or rational essence of humans. Kant, reacting to Hume before him, famously claims that arithmetic is an example of *a priori* synthetic knowledge. This means that its truth is ascertained not by verifying anything in experience, which would make it *a posteriori*, and that compared to analytic claims like "all bachelors are unmarried" in which the truth claim can be verified through the definition of the subject, Kant (1999) claims that $5 + 7 = 12$, for example, is a more complex operation (sec. B15–16). There have been subsequent philosophers who have argued that Kant is wrong and mathematics is in fact an analytic *a priori* but my interest here isn't in retracing these arguments. Rather, whether synthetic or analytic, the work of the late Wittgenstein is based upon arguing that the individual himself isn't the one who can verify the truth of mathematics. Where Kant argues that the study of philosophy is in understanding the conditions that make my individual experience possible—what he calls transcendental argumentation—Wittgenstein implies that transcendental arguments properly exist at the level of a language-speaking community.

Wittgenstein's claim is that at no point in the example of arithmetic does the mind deal with the logical essence of numbers or do any more than "blindly obey" a rule or perform a practice. In the first section of the *Investigations* Wittgenstein (2001) uses the mundane example of a child being sent to the grocer's to get five red apples. He emphasises that "the meaning of the word 'five'" never came into play, "only how the word 'five' is used" (sec. 1). In other words, the child used the practice of counting and it is in this practice that the word "five" has meaning. "Five" is to be produced by counting or through arithmetic as opposed to "hanging in the air" as some mental entity. "It is a property of this number that this process leads to it", Wittgenstein (1983) writes; "it is the end of a process (is itself part of the process)" (sec. 84). This means that I have memorised the sum $2 + 2 = 4$ but when it comes to a larger number such as $67256 + 29748$, for example, I must either "carry" on paper or "carry" in my head in order to get the sum because there is no intuitional or phenomenal access to mathematical operations which will give me the answer.[2] I "blindly obey" the practice and having signifiers for the numbers allows me to do the practice (i.e., carry the one after nine) to calculate bigger numbers. There is mathematical certainty, Wittgenstein acknowledges, but it comes from everyone ending up with the same results, once they have been made able to follow the rule, as opposed to some individual intellectual intuition.[3] Therefore this isn't a transcendental argument for how an individual possesses a rational understanding in a synthetic process. Instead, the transcendental process is moved to the level of the community of language-speaking beings and occurs through the consensus there that the rule people obey doesn't yield them different results in a way that is consistently different. A person learning arithmetic might make some errors before he follows it properly but his errors are idiosyncratic and don't offer a different logic that rivals the rule.

At this point it is important to note that Wittgenstein isn't giving an argument for cultural relativism. Just because our culture uses a decimal base and another culture might use a numerical base of six before they carry the one, doesn't mean that they have a different arithmetic than we do. Although anthropologists have found primitive political-economies in which the community might only count up to seven, for example, this only shows that mathematics hasn't been developed there, and no evidence has been found of a different form of arithmetic. Wittgenstein (2001) explicitly holds that it is "not agreement in opinions" within a community, "but in *form of life*", or our shared psychological make-up, upon which logic rests (sec. 241, emphasis mine).

Wittgenstein also considers his philosophy of language a form of therapy because he recognises that certain mathematicians or philosophers have a psychological defence in place that makes them need to believe that there is something more that they grasp in their mind.[4] To this end he compels us to pay attention to the use of language:

> "Understanding a word": a state. But a *mental* state? ... we say
> "He was depressed the whole day."
> "He was in great excitement the whole day."
> "He has been in continuous pain since yesterday."
> We also say "Since yesterday I have understood this word."
> "Continuously" though? (Wittgenstein, 2001, p. 50)

This quotation illustrates the primacy of sensation, or the experience of emotions, feelings, etc. for Wittgenstein that I will return to when I look at Kant's inscrutability claim. However, its importance here is to show that our use of language betrays that continuous experience is not on the side of logic. We don't say "I have been understanding long division since grammar school", but rather, "I've been able to do long division since ..." or "I learned long division ..." for example. Our use of language puts the experience of "Being" on the side of feeling and doesn't recognise it in the domain of logic. Wittgenstein (2001) argues that this is because the latter is only rule-following based upon "being made able to do it" (sec. 385). An adult can speak fluently without having ever formally studied language and the logic he demonstrates in his fluency is from the fact that our psychology—our minds—are built intersubjectively and connections to others create logic rather than logic issuing from a relation of the mind to itself. The problem Wittgenstein's "philosophical therapy" faces is that often philosophers have no problem abusing words or using them out of their regular sense. They may say that there is nothing wrong with "I have been understanding long division since grammar school" and that the point is communicated. Moreover, the primacy of their defence against feeling may just mean that the philosopher exchanges his view on mathematics for a physicalism that discounts all phenomenal experience (for example, DNA controls all our behaviour).

Kant's next claim enshrines the possibility of a rational essence for humanity in his notion of schematism. Kant's schematism is a return to the ancient philosophical problem of universals. The issue here is that although we can offer analytical definitions of things when we get to the "simples" or foundational parts of them, a definition is no longer possible. For example, take a red balloon. What are the conscious criteria for knowing that the balloon one sees is red? I can define the balloon as something made of plastic that is filled with air and tied to keep the air from escaping but I can't define red. Even if I can refer to the light spectrum in some way to denote it, the definition belongs to the measuring device and even someone who is colour blind can refer to the spectrum without having the qualitative experience of redness that is in question here. Past philosophers have often wanted to claim that there is a phenomenal image of redness that they can picture in their mind and this image allows them to know that something is red or not. This inner image or intuition of the universal is still involved in Kant's schematism, although in order to differentiate himself from earlier forms of idealism, he requires that the inner universal must be paired with sensible intuitions (i.e., schematised) in order for understanding to occur. "Thoughts without content are empty", he famously writes, and "intuitions without concepts are blind. The understanding can intuit nothing, the senses can think nothing. Only through their unison can knowledge arise" (Kant, 1999, sec. A51/B75).

Wittgenstein, like other philosophers, disputes that there is any inner image that somehow represents any shade of red that can be called to mind. Rather, he wants to make a separation between thinking and meaning. "Thinking" for him belongs to psychology and universals such as red come from the agreement of judgement in our "form of life."[5] When it comes to the individual mind and meaning, Wittgenstein invokes what he calls the private language argument to indicate that even if one grants an inner image of redness that indicates correspondence to every external instance of red, the problem of meaning still exists. The problem is that such an inner image is "private" and one must figure out how other people use the word red in order to use the word oneself and communicate meaning. Even if the image of a universal does phenomenally exist, or if there was some "intellectual intuition", Wittgenstein (2001) observes that "the rules [for its application] would hang in the air; for the institution of their use is lacking" (sec. 380). Different languages exist and if there were an internal image of redness, it isn't attached to a word. Therefore, if one must figure out what others mean by a word, to understand its use, then this makes the internal image superfluous to the understanding of meaning.

In the *Philosophical Investigations* Wittgenstein (2001) gives an example that helps to understand what he means here:

> suppose you came as an explorer into an unknown country with a language quite strange to you. In what circumstances would you say that the people there gave orders, understood them, obeyed them, rebelled against them, and so on? The common behaviour of mankind is the system of reference by means of which we interpret an unknown language. (Wittgenstein, 2001, sec. 206)

If you imagine yourself sharing dinner with an indigenous tribe in some unknown country and you see a few bowls of liquid on the table it would be by seeing how they are used by others (i.e., they drink it, or clean their hands in it, etc.) that the object would take on some significance to you. You would be able to signify it by paying attention to the gestures people make towards it and paying attention to the word that seems to be used only in reference to the bowl of liquid. For example they might say "Could you please pass the X", "Could you please pass the Y" and knowing the words they use in common with other objects at the table helps you to eliminate some of the possibilities. Seeing another person drink from the bowl one can understand it is something edible (i.e., be aware of the bowl of liquid as drink). Additionally, as Wittgenstein points out in the example, the bowl of liquid will be embedded in the custom of dinner and will reference etiquette, and etiquette will reference differences in rank and individual power. For example, it might be polite to let the elders at the table drink from the bowls first. An individual also might not have any higher rank than others but be feared and others may give him first choice at the table or ingratiate themselves to him by offering him many dishes. The explorer will make a prediction that a certain word is the right one to refer to the bowl of liquid, and that will be the correct sign if it results in someone gesturing to it or passing it. Moreover, once the explorer gets to understand the people better he may have the chance to decide whether or not he wants the good graces of the elders and will wait for them to drink from the bowl first. However, in transgression of etiquette we can also imagine his hosts may also decide that he's not a peer of theirs and he may have to take his meals outside of the huts or he may be seen as a witch.

Wittgenstein (2001) begins the *Investigations* by criticising Augustine's account of regarding a child as a little explorer who "could already think, only not yet speak" with think meaning "something like 'talking to itself'" (sec. 32). To regard the child as a little explorer presupposes the child is already an atomistic rational chooser while the existence of feral children illustrates that the child will not go on to invent language without the drive relations between itself and other humans. A child may possess some signs that come from its parents, who signify its desires or feelings for it, but the externally motivated achievement of the sign references the critical point of drive relatedness in which the the child forms an image-ego and needs others to think it is good. This is the base upon which language can arise as a tool. Lacan (1998) suggests that the practice of counting appears through regarding oneself from the place of the other and is betrayed in naive mistakes, like when a "simpleton" counts himself among the brothers he has—"I have three brothers Paul, Ernest, and Me" (p. 20). I'll return to this again shortly when I discuss Wittgenstein's thoughts on the origins of language.

The "common behaviour of mankind", which Wittgenstein indicates as the reference to meaning, requires that the explorer finds out how to use such words as angry, sad, confident, shy, etc. in the language of the natives. While most people will rightly dispute the internal image of redness or some platonic form of chairness, that we can conjure before our mind's eye to match, there are in fact qualitative feelings of anger, sadness, fear, etc. that we experience. We experience pain, pleasure or what can be called emotional qualia in what Wilhelm Reich (1973b) calls "organ sensations" such as the stomach "knotting" in fear, "melting" sensations in love, the heart reaching out in longing, belly laughter, (etc.). However, it is clear that we don't teach someone what a word means by referring to how the "butterflies in their stomach" feel like they are gathering to the left side, in one feeling, and the right, in another. "Introspection can never lead to a definition" as Wittgenstein (1991) puts it, "it can only lead to a psychological statement about the introspector" (Wittgenstein, 1991, sec. 212). Sensation language must still come from the outside, through actively looking for the outward expression of it or through the empathy of a caregiver who judges one is having a certain sensation and names it.[6] In this way it is clear that empathy isn't something mysterious but something normal which is at the foundation for sensation language.[7] Wittgenstein (2001) clearly shows this to be the import of the private language argument:

> now, what about the language which describes my inner experi-
> ences and which only I myself can understand? *How* do I use
> words to stand for my sensations?—As we ordinarily do? Then are
> my words tied up with my natural expressions of sensations? In
> that case my language is not a "private" one. Someone else might
> understand it as well as I. (Wittgenstein, 1991, sec. 256)

Since my private sensations can't provide a basis for me using a sign correctly, or following the rule of its public use, the fact that sensation words exist shows that there are individuals who can know the feelings, motivations, etc. of others. The words could arise from nothing else. Just as there are differences in IQ there are also differences in EQ that Wittgenstein (2001) relates to "expert judgment", with those who possess little of it being called *aspect-blind* (p. 179, 182). At the bottom of the scale there are people who can only recognise hunger, sexuality, and basic needs as "driving" some of the behaviour of others. Then, in line with many academic theories, the idea of the will to power or egoism may be taken into account with the idea of wanting recognition, "to be on top", revenge, or to have a legacy in one's children or in lasting fame.

The recognition of both egoistic and altruistic drives, as I mentioned in Chapter One always seems to be denied and to escape formalisation. I will return to this one-sided form of thinking again, but for now I want to consider the community of those with EQ.

Among those who possess EQ and have everyday conversations about how someone was very embarrassed at the meeting, how someone is pretending that his recent break up doesn't bother him but it clearly does, or that someone is "fake" and only pretending to be nice, sensation words must communicate meaning. Wittgenstein (2001), locates this meaning in shared observation of the physical expression in a third party:

> if there were for instance no characteristic expression of pain, of fear, of joy; if rule became exception and exception rule; or if both became phenomena of roughly equal frequency—this would make our normal language games lose their point. (Wittgenstein, 2001, sec. 142)

Even though one may go on to be isolated or surrounded by others of low EQ, the initial shared judgement is central. After this initial consensus Wittgenstein (2001) holds that "I can be certain of someone else's sensation as of any fact" (p. 190).[8] Although Wittgenstein focuses a lot on just simple sensations such as pain or joy for the benefit of his aspect-blind philosophical audience he does give some more complicated examples that point to more complicated instances of motivations and different "attitudes" that aren't mere sensation or biological instinct like hunger or sexuality. For example, he writes:

> there is such a thing as guessing thoughts in the sense that someone says to me: "I know what you have just thought" (or "What you just thought of") and I have to admit that he has guessed my thoughts right .... And wouldn't this too be conceivable: I tell someone "You have just thought ... to yourself"—He denies it. But I stick to my assertion, and in the end he says: "I believe you are right; I must have thought that to myself; my memory must be deceiving me." And now imagine this being a quite ordinary episode! ... "Thoughts and feelings are private." means roughly the same as "There is pretending," or "One can hide one's thoughts and feelings; can even lie and dissimulate." And the question is, what is the import of this "There is ..." and "One can". (Wittgenstein, 1991, sec. 568–570)[9]

Wittgenstein recognises that even people with high EQ can make mistakes and lying and dissimulation exist, but calls us to recognise that there are cases of someone attempting to lie that someone with EQ can judge to be lying and force to "come clean".[10] In a related example, the body can effectively "lie" and cover up the physical expression of an emotion. Although emotions are often simple to see in children, in many adults full sobbing, for example, may be replaced by being "choked up" or "misty eyed" in sadness and only include a portion of the original physical response. Wilhelm Reich (1990) went beyond proverbial character armour in the personality to the observation that chronic muscular tensions constitute a literal armour. Reich's work overcomes the residue of Cartesian dualism still left in psychoanalysis and shows that repression isn't a mere banishment of an "idea" but, since it involves emotion, there must also be the physical *suppression* of it. The realms of Being that I sketched in Chapter Three are often displayed and referenced in the individual's physical comportment. For example, tight assed, stiff necked, the unsure grounding of a "push over", etc. are linked to certain character types and will no doubt help explain some of the symbols in many myths.

For those without enough EQ it's doubtful that Wittgenstein's transcendental argument or Reich's explanation for the variety of emotional responses will satisfy. However, it's possible to also make an existential argument in which one appeals to the social power of certain individuals who display their expert judgement. The aspect-blind person can be directed to the reputation that certain people in the community have for their "good sense", wisdom, or ability to make those feeling emotional hurt, or defending against it, return once again to their work or love-life. Additionally, conmen who have been able to marry woman after woman and defraud them, or pull off complex crimes also illustrate this ability. I think that it is much more realistic to think that the aspect-blind may possibly come to grips with their lack of EQ not through trying to discover it in their own phenomenal experience but by seeing the outcomes of its use by others. Regardless, it is interesting to feel Wittgenstein (1991) lose patience with the patients of his philosophical therapy:

> "I can only believe that someone else is in pain, but I know it if I am"—Yes: one can make the decision to say "I believe he is in pain" instead of "He is in pain." But that is all ... Just try—in a real case— to doubt someone else's fear or pain. (Wittgenstein, 1991, sec. 303)

Just try to reflect on something very sad with an expression of radiant joy. (Wittgenstein, 1991, sec. 801)

Because introspection can never lead to a definition, when, through an act of mimicry, one comes to empathise with what another is feeling and can name it, Wittgenstein holds that EQ is also a logical operation. He writes:

we react to the visual impression differently from someone who does not recognize it as timid (in the full sense of the word).—But I do *not* want to say here that we feel this reaction in our muscles and joints and that this is the 'sensing'.—No, what we have here is a modified concept of *sensation* ... This is, of course, not simply a question for physiology. Here the physiological is a symbol of the logical ... . It is almost as if there were a face there which at first I *imitate*, and then accept without imitating it. (Wittgenstein, 2001, p. 179)

Along with mimicry allowing one to know someone is happy, sad, in pain, etc. from an initial shared observation of the behaviour of the particular feeling with someone else in a third person, or from one's parents having given signification to one's own emotional reactions, more complex character traits must also be signified beyond the experience of qualia.[11] In addition to perceiving "timidity" Wittgenstein (2001) also asks us how "the feeling of confidence is ... manifested in behaviour" and notes that the aspect-blind person may ask "What is confidence?" or "Can someone be almost confident, or half confident?" (sec. 579).

In the chapter on "psychic bisexuality" I pointed out that certain cultures might encourage egoism but that the individual character trait of ambitiousness, will still be discernable because the individual will be more egoistic than the norm. The ambitious person's economic emphasis on jealousy and needing to have a potent reputation will drive him to do more than the norm in the culture (or force a defence against this drive). The ambitious person in this example, or the confident person in Wittgenstein's, must be judged in comparison to others and over time so that individual actions can be judged to be traits. Then, once the individual with high EQ has a logical sense of the interrelations of many others, it is possible that he or she can accurately judge another person to be cocky or impressed with himself by his physical comportment without the need for studying his behaviour over a long course of time. The ancients had such expressions as "Speak so that I may see thee" that denote judging certain character traits from voice, physical comportment, or physiognomy. Again, this goes along with the caveats that everyone has their blind spots.

In the chapter on psychic bisexuality I mentioned that liberals often have to believe that "deep down" that people are good or really care about others despite ample evidence for the contrary. In the last chapter I indicated that Fairbairn observed the defence of melancholia to be necessary for feeling that father-substitutes, and the reality functions related to them, are good because to see them as bad would be too frightening to someone who is driven by the need for their approval. So, even in the altruists who are disposed to higher EQ—as well as those with early schizoid fixations that encourage the exchange of cultural pursuits for relationships—blind spots are built into their character. The over-coming of these blind spots, not just in the realm of thought but in one's embodied or face-to face meetings with people, provides, I believe, the best notion of Nietzsche's hope for the ubermensch who is more than a "free spirit" or isolated, ghost-like thinker.

Along with the observable power of the wise person and the con-man, the existence of many different feeling and motivation words are regarded as capturing fine distinctions between different psychological types and can't simply be exchanged. For the person of good judgement being angry, furious, irritated, livid, enraged, etc. aren't interchangeable. Wittgenstein (2001) writes:

> we speak of understanding a sentence in the sense in which it can be replaced by another which says the same; but also in the sense in which it cannot be replaced by any other. (Any more than one musical theme can be replaced by another). In the one case the thought in the sentence is something common to different sentences; in the other, something that is expressed only by these words in these positions. (Understanding a poem.) .... Then has "understanding" two different meanings here?—I would rather say that these kinds of use of "understanding" make up its meaning, make up my *concept* of understanding. For I *want* to apply the word "understanding" to all this. (Wittgenstein, 2001, sec. 531, 532).
>
> The familiar physiognomy of a word, the feeling that it has taken up its meaning into itself, that it is an actual likeness of its meaning—there could be human beings to whom all this was alien.

(They would not have an attachment to their words.)—And how are these feelings manifested by us?—By the way we choose and value words. (Wittgenstein, 2001, p. 186)

To some extent Wittgenstein is saying that those with small vocabularies lack EQ or at least can't communicate it, but a large vocabulary doesn't necessarily mean that one has it either, because one could be pretentious and misuse words. Shared judgement between people of wisdom is the only measure here and often wisdom expressed in art, for example, can only be verified by the public long after the death of an artist, when his work is shown to have staying power. Interestingly, Wittgenstein's indications of the physiognomy of words—their feeling right or wrong as descriptors in a certain case—which, either references physiognomy or the aptness of metaphor in relation to unconscious phantasy, is a reversal of "intellectual intuition". It doesn't concern universals or arithmetic that concern some inner rational essence but relate to our primarily related, social essence.

Without the need for an intellectual intuition in arithmetic or an inner/private criterion of correctness for signs, Kant's categorical imperative as an operation that the inner rational self chooses loses its grounding. Although Kant recognises both egoistic and altruistic drives, the division he makes between the sensible world with drives or inclinations (phenomenal) and the world of understanding that is governed by the categorical imperative (noumenal) effectively robs any confidence from judgement of motivations (Kant, 2002, sec. 4:457).[12] For Kant, the categorical imperative is the claim that the possible rational essence of humanity, enshrined in the antinomies, may cause us to act with respect for the rational will of others so that we don't perform an action that all other rational beings can't perform if it leads to a contradiction. A famous example is lying. If I lie and imagine that all other people will lie too then no one can be trusted to keep their promises, nor trust me, and my action of lying couldn't be efficacious and thus is contradictory. In Kant's system "bad" actions always issue from inclinations but one has the choice to act on a bad inclination or not, and it isn't possible to tell if a good action is based upon phenomenal drives or has been willed through the noumenal categorical imperative. Wittgenstein's recognition of arithmetic as rule-following, which must be corroborated by the community, attacks the foundation of arithmetic being derived from individual synthetic *a priori* reason. An individual can "do math" or perform a calculation but can't provide his own criterion of correctness, and must rely upon others producing the same answer as proof of its correctness. After checking with others a sufficient amount of time she can have some confidence in the calculations without checking, but this allegedly synthetic *a priori* doesn't issue from an individual's reason providing its own criterion of correctness and therefore can't provide an analogy for reason seeing the correctness of the categorical imperative.

Kant's account requires a noumenal lacunae in which reason can verify itself so as to doubt phenomenal motivations. If epistemology doesn't require the synthetic *a priori* or the schematism then the large number of feeling and motivation words, which also must be derived from observation, and can't be confused with arising from private sensation or experience, suggest the noumenal lacunae is superfluous. As noted in Chapter Two, a categorical imperative type of operation may occur with imagos, but there is no reason to suggest that it is willed or chosen by some rational essence. Instead of the categorical imperative being a choice of "pure reason", Freud's conception of the superego, which is anchored in observable pathology and tensions, locates it first in the relation and respect for the father imago. However, it is possible one can defuse from the father imago and not show remorse for acting unfairly with others. Then, when the imago undergoes the modification in the father complex, it is established as a permanent self-observation. Irrational feelings of guilt observed in some people's pathology can be understood in a dynamic model, and to return to dualism once more means that understanding and treatment is sacrificed for egotism.

There is one final implications of Wittgenstein's private language argument. It forces us to recognise a pre-historic ground zero point of culture in which the ego and object drives and superego alone determine the motivations of human beings and therefore provide a basis of human behaviour for the sensation signs to be attached to. Wittgenstein (1970) writes:

> being sure that someone is in pain, doubting whether he is, and so on, are so many natural instinctive kinds of behaviour towards other human beings, and our language is merely an auxiliary to, and further extension of, this relation. Our language-game is an extension of primitive behaviour. (For our *language-game* is behaviour) (Instinct). (Wittgenstein, 1970, sec. 545)

I want to regard man here as an animal; as a primitive being to which one grants instinct but not ratiocination. As a creature in a primitive state. Any logic good enough for a primitive means of communication needs no apology from us. Language did not emerge from some kind of ratiocination. (Wittgenstein, 1969, sec. 475)

In other words, as the third chimpanzee went about getting food and navigating the social hierarchy of its group, language began to emerge as a tool. In Chapter Three I mentioned the phallic image-ego of wanting to be admired for doing something well. Although it is connected to one's reputation, and reputation can be conveyed by language, language isn't necessary. Reputation can be communicated through holding the attention of others and indications of deference or awe from others can be taken from their body language. Language would only extend the drive that underpins this and it's possible to imagine it rising from different desires. For example, the desire to boast about what one did when others weren't there to see. As I quoted above, language-games themselves are auxiliaries to other forms of drives, and although we can't know exactly how language arose we can imagine many different motivations for it. Wanting to hear about some exciting change in the social hierarchy one wasn't there to witness, for example, or to communicate one's love, mourning, and desire to keep the memory of the beloved who was lost alive show the practical use for language. The key is that it is only with the rise of the phallic image ego that the egoist becomes connected enough to others (through the ego and object drives) to pay attention to what they notice and how they behave to construct a theory of mind.

There is a dialectic between different ways of striving for happiness (power vs. belonging) and the social ideals introduced in the father complex and elaborated in latency. The different forms of thought that fail to recognise this can be assessed as making mystical, relativistic, or mechanistic errors. The first is based upon whether they ignore the social creation of signs and derive the will from an intellectual intuition of rational essence, or conscience, and feeling from introspection. The second accepts cultural inputs only and doesn't recognise that signs must arise from established behaviours in the individual drive-based motivation system. The third issues from the denial of the importance of consciousness of motivations or the existence of logic in practices like arithmetic or science.

The *mystics* appeal to a subjective absolute human freedom through reason or through the conscience, or claim to have unique feelings that they alone can only understand. In the first case they appeal to the freedom of the will in reason as if it is a metaphysical fact that they have direct access to. Following Nietzsche (2000), I've recognised that ideas come to mind when *they* want, and there's no connection to, or intuition for, any inner, rational self. This version of the mystic appeals to universals, arithmetic, and the necessity of individual criteria of correctness in epistemology to support an atomistic rational being. In the second case a mystic may appeal to a metaphysical eternal moral order in the subjective experience of the conscience. However, they do so as if different religions, moral orders, and revelations didn't exist from culture to culture and without recognition of the "irrational" functioning of the conscience in mental disorders. In the third case, the mystic may claim her feelings are unique and that words can't express them or that others can't know how she feels. The mystical errors here fall short of observing the importance of "the sign" and go back to an atomism that invents the internal universal, or reifies the qualia, so that a solipsistic world view becomes possible. The intersubjective creation of the mind is denied and mental illness and such facts as feral children not forming any language are seen as mere chemical or bodily problems that have nothing to do with the indivisible mind.

The relativistic errors either move these same problems to a reification of culture or deny the judgement of individual motivations altogether in their assertions. For example, instead of the metaphysical claim of the freedom of choice from reason, the same indivisibility of the mind exists, but the relativistic claim is that cultural values are inscribed in the individual and that they determine what he will do. The values of a certain historical culture make him egoistic, for example, and any individual differences in character occur from different "narratives" the individual has internalised. Narratives have primacy and atomistic individuals overcome their primary separateness through linguistically mediated narratives. There are also relativists who reify culture so that we are told that every culture is unique and they are impossible for us to understand or empathise with their members. This reification can again be understood as the transferring the uniqueness of feeling from the individual to the cultural level. In addition, there are ethical relativists who don't recognise development in ethical life or the trans-historical status of the phallic and pre-phallic superego. Like the mystic claiming that his religion is the only true one, the relativist claims that pluralism is eternal and doesn't recognise the individual psychology that culture is anchored in. He doesn't see how political-economy and having a certain amount of technology and division of labour to support a certain class structure will produce similar values in geographically isolated cultures. All these views fail to recognise the ground zero point of culture and the necessity of attaching signs to emotional and drive-based behaviour. Superego prohibitions that come from the imago or latency superego values that come from a certain political-economy are denied, and the *ex-nihilo* creation of cultural values (*contra* Kroeber) and practices (*contra* Roheim) illustrates how relativists are just mystics at the level of culture and lose sight of civilisation.

Lastly, there are mechanists who deny both subjective experience and the input of culture. Although, ironically, they have no problem making use of them to make their arguments. They essentially make human beings into automatons of their DNA and evolutionary instincts, or may recognise repetition-compulsions in behaviour but claim that it is a mere learned behaviour or conditioning from childhood and disregard the imago or intersubjective process. There are also irrationalists who deny the development of the practices of logic in civilisation. To be certain, the advancement of civilisation doesn't necessarily mean more emotional health and, to the extent that word culture represents the attempt to note that less sophisticated political-economies can have more health than more sophisticated ones, there is an important point here. The irrationalists reify culture to claim that science or calculus is equal to the mysticism found in primitive political-economies. They don't appeal to culture evidence but simply claim that mathematics and logic are illusory. They belong in this category since their position appears as a negation of the standard mechanistic account of the world, in that the mechanists use logic and mathematics to create their arguments.

Again, I'm aware that many people have developed the views I have presented in more subtle ways. However, the subtlety of some of these views aren't often understood by their adherents. This appendix serves to dispel some of the gross mischaracterisations and, at the same time, show the ground of a sufficient view that recognises individual character, motivations, and has a place for individual psychology amongst the processes that occur in civilisation (i.e., the development of political-economy) and the values that exist in an individual culture.

Notes

1. Such character defences have been approached from the angle of defusion from the father imago and are the same as those represented by Reich (1990) but can also include more than the "defence" against taking a father-substitute in one's ego ideal. For example, they can include the further paranoiac or melancholic defences, projective identification in which one repeats the position of the father imago while another person repeats the position the ego would normally. For example, in the primal scene trauma/fixation, the egoist finds that his mother had "betrayed" him by having sex with his father. If activated later in life the individual may find himself cheated on, cuckholded, or similarly "betrayed" by his current object. However, he may also assume the position of the father imago and seek objects in which he will create the "injured third party."

2. "Ask yourself: Would it be imaginable for someone to learn to do sums in his head without ever doing written or oral ones?—'Learning it' will mean: **being made able to** do it" (Wittgenstein, 2001, sec. 385, **emphasis** added).

3. "Mathematicians don't quarrel over the result of a calculation. (This is an important fact.).—If it were otherwise, if for instance one mathematician was convinced that a figure had altered unperceived, or that his or someone else's memory had been deceived, and so on—then our concept of 'mathematical certainty' would not exist … True we can never *know* what the result of a calculation is, but for all that it always has a quite definite result … But am I trying to say some such thing as that the certainty of mathematics is based on the reliability of ink and paper? *No.* (That would be a vicious circle.)—I have not said why mathematicians do not quarrel, but only *that* they do not" (Wittgenstein, 2001, p. 192).

4. "… We have to give a psychologically exact account of the temptation to use a particular kind of expression. What we 'are tempted to say' in such a case is, of course, not philosophy; but it is its raw material. Thus, for example, what a mathematician is inclined to say about the objectivity and reality of mathematical facts, is not a philosophy of mathematics, but something for philosophical treatment" (Wittgenstein, 2001, sec. 254).

5. "If language is to be a means of communication there must be agreement not only in definitions but also (queer as this may sound) in judgments" (Wittgenstein, 2001, p. 242). "There is such a thing as colour-blindness and there are ways of establishing it. There is in general complete agreement in the judgments of colours made by those diagnosed who have been diagnosed normal" (ibid., p. 193).

6. "Now do I learn the meaning of the word 'sad'—as applied to a face—in just the same way as the meaning of 'round' or 'red'? No, not in quite the same way, but still in a similar way. (I do also react differently to a face's sadness ...)" (Wittgenstein, 1991, sec. 1071).

7. Wittgenstein (1991) repeats himself again and again with many little remarks that try to show the existence of empathy: "[o]ne may note an alteration in a face and describe it by saying that the face assumed a harder expression—and yet not be able to describe the alteration in spatial terms. This is enormously important (sec. 919). 'How does one realize that the expression of joy is not the expression of some bodily pain? (An *important* question)' (sec. 858). 'I see that the child wants to touch the dog, but doesn't dare.' How can I see that? ... remember that you may also mimic a human being who would like to touch something, but doesn't dare" (sec. 1066).

8. The same thing goes with IQ innovations. Someone who comes up with a new "game", invention, or theory that comes to be accepted can understand it before the community accepts it. I feel the need to point this out because such naïve interpretations of Wittgenstein exist although he clearly speaks against them: "as things are I can, for example, invent a game that is never played by anyone.—But would the following be possible too: mankind has never played any games; once, however, someone invented a game—which no one ever played?" (Wittgenstein, 2001, sec. 204). However, after one has the initial consensus and goes on to independent judgements it is possible that being disagreed with by others who one respects as having EQ can lead to doubts and loss of confidence.

9. Wittgenstein (2001) gives an example in the investigation of catching someone in a lie that should help illustrate the guessing of someone's thoughts: "but can't one also lie in this way: one says 'It'll stop soon', and means pain—but when asked 'What did you mean?' one answers 'The noise in the next room?' In this sort of case one might say: 'I was going to answer ... but thought better of it and did not answer ...'" (Wittgenstein, 2001, sec. 668).

10. "It is certainly possible to be convinced by evidence that someone is in such and such a state of mind, that for instance, he is not pretending. But 'evidence' here includes 'imponderable' evidence ... include[ing]

subtleties of glance, of gesture, or tone. I may recognize a genuine loving look, distinguish it from a pretended one (and here there can, of course, be a 'ponderable' confirmation of my judgment). But I may be quite incapable of describing the difference …—if I were a very talented painter I might conceivably represent the genuine and the simulated glance in pictures" (Wittgenstein, 2001, p. 194).

11. To be clear, once the child has enough shared observations of the emotional state of a third person with others, it can go on to observe others on its own and, for example, have a bigger vocabulary then others in her social circles. The child can read books and figure out how to apply the right emotional words or character traits to the people that it knows without the corroboration of others. The child may actually go on to apply the word mistakenly and may eventually meet someone who corrects its use of it but, Wittgenstein isn't saying that everyone in a culture must play the same "language-games" but only that the initial shared judgement is necessary. Wittgenstein (2001) writes, "[a]s things are I can, for example, invent a game that is never played by anyone.— But would the following be possible too: mankind has never played any games; once, however, someone invented a game—which no one ever played?" (PI-204).

12. Along with the example of a shopkeeper who may act from the categorical imperative or may be acting from the self interest of having a good reputation, Kant also recognises altruistic motivations. He writes, "to be beneficent where one can is a duty, and besides there are some souls so sympathetically attuned that, even without any other motive of vanity or utility to self, that take an inner gratification in spreading joy around them, and can take delight in the contentment of others insofar as it is their own work. But I assert that in such a case the action, however it may conform to duty and however amiable it is, nevertheless has no true moral worth, but is on the same footing with other inclinations, e.g., the inclination to honour, which, when it fortunately encounters something that in fact serves the common good and is in conformity with duty, and is thus worthy of honour, deserves praise and encouragement, but no esteem; for the maxim lacks moral content, namely of doing such actions not from inclination but *from duty*" (Kant, 2002, sec. 4:398). Kant criticises these drives because a person may have misfortunes befall him and lose these inclinations and, ultimately, although he may be moral all his life it comes from luck that nothing horrible happened to him. However, Kant doesn't recognise the possibility that his preoccupation with morality may itself be defensive and involve egoistic masochism.

REFERENCES

Abraham, K. (1922). Manifestations of the female castration complex. *International Journal Psycho-Analysis, 3*: 1–29.

Abraham, K. (1923). Contributions to the theory of the anal character. *International Journal Psycho-Analysis, 4*: 400–418.

Abraham, K. (1926). Character-formation on the genital level of libido-development. *International Journal Psycho-Analysis, 7*: 214–222.

Adler, A. (1946). *Individual Psychology.* (P. Radin, Trans.). London: Kegan Paul, Trench, Trubner & Co.

Anzieu, D. (1987). Some alterations of the ego which make analyses interminable. *International Journal Psycho-Analysis, 68*: 9–19.

Becker, E. (1973). *Denial of Death.* USA: Free Press Paperbacks, 1997.

Bergler, E., & Herzman, A. (1944). On a clinical approach to the psychoanalysis of writers. *The Psychoanalytic Review, 31*: 40–70.

Bernstein, J. S. (1975–1976). The autistic character. The *Psychoanalytic Review, 62*: 537–555.

Blackburn, M. (2013). www.dailykos.com/story/2013/11/01/1252250/-Jon-Stewart-blasts-Republicans-for-sheer-idiocy-in-Obamacare-hearings# Last accessed 15 August 2014.

Blatt, S. J. (1998). Contributions of psychoanalysis to the understanding and treatment of depression. *Journal American Psychoanalysis Association, 46*: 723–752.

Brenner, C. (1994). The mind as conflict and compromise formation. *Journal of Clinical Psychoanalysis, 3*: 473–488.

Brunswick, R. M. (1940). The preoedipal phase of the libido development. *Psychoanalytic Quarterly, 9*: 293–319.

Chasseguet-Smirgel, J. (1974). Perversion, idealization and sublimation. *International Journal Psycho-Analysis, 55*: 349–357.

Chasseguet-Smirgel, J. (1976a). Freud and female sexuality—The consideration of some blind spots in the exploration of the "Dark Continent". *International Journal Psycho-Analysis, 57*: 275–286.

Chasseguet-Smirgel, J. (1976b). Some thoughts on the ego ideal a contribution to the study of the "Illness of ideality". *Psychoanalysis Quarterly, 45*: 345–373.

Cohen, M., & Armelagos, G. (Eds.). (1984). *Paleopathology at the Origins of Agriculture*. USA: Academic Press.

Coriat, I. H. (1924). The character traits of urethral erotism. *The Psychoanaytic Review, 11*: 426–434.

Davis, H. L. (1965–1966). Short-term psychoanalytic therapy with hospitalized schizophrenics. *The Psychoanaytic. Review, 52D*: 81–108.

Davis, P. *et al* (Producer), & Mulcahy, R. (Director). (1986). *Highlander* [Motion Picture]. United Kingdom, United States: Twentieth Century Fox.

Deutsch, H. (1930). The significance of masochism in the mental life of women. *International Journal Psycho-Analysis, 11*: 48–60.

Deutsch, H. (1973). *The Psychology of Women* (two volumes). New York: Grune & Stratton; Bantam Books. (Originally published in 1945).

Easser, B. R., & Lesser, S. R. (1965). Hysterical personality: A re-evaluation. *The Psychoanaytic Quarterly, 34*: 390–405.

Eigen, M. (1995). Psychic Deadness: Freud. *Contemporary Psychoanalysis, 31*: 277.

Elias, N. (1994). *The Civilizing Process*, Malden, USA: Blackwell Publishers.

Elkin, H. (1972). On Selfhood and the Development of Ego Structures in Infancy. Psychoanal. Rev., 59: 389–416.

Erikson, E. (1963). *Childhood and Society*, USA: W. W. Norton & Co, 1978.

Fairbairn, W. R. D. (1952). *Psychoanalytic Studies of the Personality*. London: Tavistock Publications Limited.

Falzeder, E., & Brabant, E. (1996). *The Correspondence of Sigmund Freud and Sándor Ferenczi, Volume 2, 1914–1919*. Cambridge, MA/London: The Belknap Press of Harvard University Press.

Fenichel, O. (1938). Ego-disturbances and their treatment. *International Journal Psycho-Analysis, 19*: 416–438.

Fenichel, O. (1944). Psychoanalytic remarks on Fromm's book "Escape from Freedom". *The Psychoanalytic Review, 31*: 133–152.

Ferenczi, S. (1925). Psycho-analysis of sexual habits. *International Journal Psycho-Analysis, 6*: 372–404.

Fink, B. (1995). *The Lacanian Subject: Between Language and Jouissance.* Princeton, NJ: Princeton University Press.

Fink, B. (1997). *A Clinical Introduction to Lacanian Psychoanalysis: Theory and Technique.* USA: Harvard University Press.

Freud, S. (1905a). Jokes and their relation to the unconscious. *S. E., 8*: 1–247. London: Hogarth.

Freud, S. (1905b). Three essays on the theory of sexuality. *S. E., 7*: 123–246. London: Hogarth.

Freud, S. (1908). "Civilized" sexual morality and modern nervous illness. *S. E., 9*: 177–204. London: Hogarth.

Freud, S. (1909). Notes upon a case of obsessional neurosis. *S. E., 10*: 151–318. London: Hogarth.

Freud, S. (1910). Leonardo Da Vinci and a memory of his childhood. *S. E., 11*: 57–138. London: Hogarth.

Freud, S. (1911a). Formulations on the two principles of mental functioning. *S. E., 12*: 213–226. London: Hogarth.

Freud, S. (1911b). Psycho-analytic notes on an autobiographical account of a case of paranoia (Dementia paranoides). *S. E., 12*: 1–82. London: Hogarth.

Freud, S. (1912). The dynamics of transference. *S. E., 12: 12*: 97–108. London: Hogarth.

Freud, S. (1913). Totem and taboo. *S. E., 13*: vii–162. London: Hogarth.

Freud, S. (1914a). On the history of the psycho-analytic movement. *S. E., 14*: 1–66. London: Hogarth.

Freud, S. (1914b). On narcissism. *S. E., 14*: 67–102. London: Hogarth.

Freud, S. (1914c). Some reflections on schoolboy psychology. *S. E., 13*: 239–244. London: Hogarth.

Freud, S. (1915). Instincts and their vicissitudes. *S. E., 14*: 109–140. London: Hogarth.

Freud, S. (1916). Some character-types met with in psycho-analytic work. *S. E., 14*: 309–333. London: Hogarth.

Freud, S. (1917a). A difficulty in the path of psycho-analysis. *S. E., 17*: 135–144. London: Hogarth.

Freud, S. (1917b). Introductory lectures on psycho-analysis. *S. E., 16*: 241–463. London: Hogarth.

Freud, S. (1917c). On transformations of instinct as exemplified in anal erotism. *S. E., 17*: 125–134. London: Hogarth.

Freud, S. (1919a). "A child is being beaten" A contribution to the study of the origin of sexual perversions. *S. E., 17*: 175–204. London: Hogarth.

Freud, S. (1919b). The "uncanny". *S. E., 17*: 217–256. London: Hogarth.

Freud, S. (1920). Beyond the pleasure principle. *S. E., 18*: 1–64. London: Hogarth.

Freud, S. (1921). Group psychology and the analysis of the ego. *S. E., 18*: 65–144. London: Hogarth.

Freud, S. (1922). Some neurotic mechanisms in jealousy, paranoia and homosexuality. *S. E., 18*: 221–232. London: Hogarth.

Freud, S. (1923a). A seventeenth-century demonological neurosis. *S. E., 19*: 67–106. London: Hogarth.

Freud, S. (1923b). The ego and the id. *S. E., 19*: 1–66. London: Hogarth.

Freud, S. (1924a). The dissolution of the Oedipus complex. *S. E., 19*: 171–180. London: Hogarth.

Freud, S. (1924b). The economic problem of masochism. *S. E., 19*: 155–170.

Freud, S. (1925). Negation. *S. E., 19*: 233–240. London: Hogarth.

Freud, S. (1926a). Inhibitions, symptoms and anxiety. *S. E., 20*: 75–176. London: Hogarth.

Freud, S. (1926b). The question of lay analysis. *S. E., 20*: 177–258. London: Hogarth.

Freud, S. (1927a). The future of an illusion. *S. E., 21*: 1–56. London: Hogarth.

Freud, S. (1927b). Humour. *S. E., 21*: 159–166. London: Hogarth.

Freud, S. (1930). Civilization and its discontents. *S. E., 21*: 57–146. London: Hogarth.

Freud, S. (1931a). Female sexuality. *S. E., 21*: 221–244. London: Hogarth.

Freud, S. (1931b). Libidinal types. *S. E., 21*: 215–220. London: Hogarth.

Freud, S. (1933). New introductory lectures on psycho-analysis. *S. E., 22*: 1–182. London: Hogarth.

Freud, S. (1937). Analysis terminable and interminable. *S. E., 23*: 209–254. London: Hogarth.

Freud, S. (1938). An outline of psycho-analysis. *S. E., 23*: 139–208. London: Hogarth.

Freud, S. (1939). Moses and monotheism. *S. E., 23*: 1–138. London: Hogarth.

Green, A. (1997). The dead mother. In: *On Private Madness* (pp. 142–173). London: Karnac (Originally published in 1986).

Grotstein, J. S. (1990). Nothingness, meaninglessness, chaos, and the "black hole" II—The black hole. *Contemporary Psychoanalysis, 26*: 377–407.

Grunberger, B. (1977). Study of anal object relations. *International Review of Psycho-Analysis, 4*: 99–110.

Hárnik, J. (1924). The various developments undergone by narcissism in men and in women. *International Journal of Psycho-Analysis, 5*: 66–83.

Hartmann, H. (1950). Comments on the psychoanalytic theory of the ego. *The Psychoanalytic Study of the Child, 5*: 74–96.

Hegel, G. F. W. (1977). *Phenomenology of Spirit.* (A. V. Miller, Trans.). USA: Oxford University Press (originally published in 1807).

Hegel, G. F. W. (1984). *Lectures on the Philosophy of World History Introduction.* (H. S. Nisbet, Trans.). New York, NY: Cambridge University Press (originally published in 1975).

Hendrick, I. (1936). Ego development and certain character problems. *The Psychoanalytic Quarterly, 5*: 320–346.

Hendrick, I. (1938). *Facts and Theories of Psychoanalysis.* NY, USA: Alfred A. Knopf, 1958.

Hendrick, I. (1943a). The discussion of the "Instinct to Master"—*A Letter to the Editors. The Psychoanalytic Quarterly., 12*: 561–565.

Hendrick, I. (1943b). Work and the pleasure principle. *The Psychoanalytic Quarterly, 12*: 311–329.

Hendrick, I. (1951). Early development of the ego: Identification in infancy. *The Psychoanaytic Quarterly, 20*: 44–61.

Horney, K. (1937). *Neurotic Personality of Our Time.* New York: W. W. Norton & Company, 1994.

Horney, K. (1950). *Neurosis and Human Growth.* New York: W. W. Norton & Company.

Hymer, S. M. (1984). Narcissistic friendships. *The Psychoanalytic Review, 71*: 423–439.

Jackson, P. *et al* (Producer), & Jackson, P. (Director). (2001). *The Fellowship of the Ring* [Motion picture]. United Kingdom, New Zealand, United States: New Line Cinema.

Jackson, P. *et al* (Producer), & Jackson, P. (Director). (2002). *The Two Towers* [Motion picture]. United Kingdom, New Zealand, United States: New Line Cinema.

Jackson, P. *et al* (Producer), & Jackson, P. (Director). (2003). *The Return of the King* [Motion picture]. United Kingdom, New Zealand, United States: New Line Cinema.

Jacobson, E. (1954a). Contribution to the metapsychology of psychotic identifications. *Journal of the American Psychoanalysis Association, 2*: 239–262.

Jacobson, E. (1954b). The self and the object world—Vicissitudes of their infantile cathexes and their influence on ideational and affective development. *The Psychoanaytic Study of the Child, 9*: 75–127.

Johnson, S. (1994). *Character Styles.* NY, USA: W. W. Norton & Company.

Jones, E. (1951). The God complex. In: *Essays in Applied Psycho-Analysis, 2* (pp. 244–265). London: Hogarth (originally published in 1913).

Jung, C. G. (1944). *Psychology and Alchemy.* Collected Works 12 (R. Hull, Trans. H. Read, M. Fordham & G. Adler, Eds.). London: Routledge and Kegan Paul. Princeton: University Press.

Kant, I. (1999). *Critique of Pure Reason*. Cambridge, UK: Cambridge University Press, 1787.

Kant, I. (2002). *Groundwork for the Metaphysics of Morals*. USA: Yale University Press, 1785.

Kardiner, A. (1939). *The Individual and His Society: The Psychodynamics of Primitive Social Organization*. NY, USA: Columbia University Press.

Kazanjian, L. (Producer), & Marquand, R. (Director). (1983). *Return of the Jedi*. [Motion Picture]. United States of America, Twentieth Century Fox Film Corporation.

Kill, A. S. (1986). Kohut's psychology of the self as model for theological dynamics. *Union Seminary Quarterly Review, 41*: 17–32.

Klein, M. (1927). The psychological principles of infant analysis. *International Journal Psycho-Analysis, 8*: 25–37.

Klein, M. (1928). Note on the preceding communication. *International Journal Psycho-Analysis, 9*: 255–258.

Klein, M. (1932). The psycho-analysis of children. *International Journal Psycho-Analysis, 22*: 1–379. London: Hogarth.

Klein, M. (1935). A contribution to the psychogenesis of manic-depressive states. *International Journal Psycho-Analysis, 16*: 145–174.

Klein, M. (1940). Mourning and its relation to manic-depressive states. *International Journal Psycho-Analysis, 21*: 125–153.

Klein, M. (1945). The Oedipus complex in the light of early anxieties. *International Journal Psycho-Analysis, 26*: 11–33.

Klein, M. (1948). A contribution to the theory of anxiety and guilt. *International Journal Psycho-Analysis, 29*: 114–123.

Klein, M. (1958). On the development of mental functioning. *International Journal Psycho-Analysis, 39*: 84–90.

Klein, M. (1975). *Envy and Gratitude and Other Works 1946–1963*. *The International Psycho-Analytic Library, 104*: 1–346. London: Hogarth and the Institute of Psycho-Analysis.

Kohut, H. (1971). *The Analysis of the Self: A Systematic Approach to the Psychoanalytic Treatment of Narcissistic Personality Disorders*. Madison, USA: International Universities Press, 1989.

Kohut, H. (1977). *The Restoration of the Self*. New York, USA: International Universities Press.

Kroeber, A. (1920). Totem and taboo: an ethnologic psycho-analysis. *American Anthropologist, 22*: 1.

Kurtz, G. (Producer), & Lucas, G. (Director). (1977). *Star Wars*. [Motion picture]. United States of America: Twentieth Century Fox Film Corporation.

Kurtz, G. (Producer), & Kershner, I. (Director). (1980). *The Empire Strikes Back*. [Motion picture]. United States of America: Twentieth Century Fox Film Corporation.

Lacan, J. (1993). *The Seminar. Book III. The Pscyhoses*, 1955–1956. (R. Grigg, Trans.). London: Routledge.

Lacan, J. (1998). The Seminar of Jacques Lacan: The Four Fundamental Concepts of Psychoanalysis (Vol. Book XI) (The Seminar of Jacques Lacan) (A. Sheridan Trans.). New York: W. W. Norton & Company, Inc.

Laplanche, J. (1999). *Essays on Otherness*. London: Routledge.

Lewes, K. (1998). A special oedipal mechanism in the development of male homosexuality. *Psychoanalytic Psychology, 15*: 341–359.

Lionells, M. (1986). A reevaluation of hysterical relatedness. *Contemporary Psychoanalysis, 22*: 570–597.

Loewald, H. W. (1951). Ego and reality. *International Journal Psycho-Analysis, 32*: 10–18.

Loewald, H. W. (1985). Oedipus complex and development of self. *The Psychoanalytic Quarterly, 54*: 435–443.

Loewenstein, R. (1935). Phallic passivity in men. *International Journal Psycho-Analysis, 16*: 334–340.

Malinowski, B. (1922). Argonauts of the Western Pacific, London: Routledge.

McGee, Jon R., Warms, Richard L. (2003). Anthropological Theory: An Introductory History 3rd Ed., New York: McGraw-Hill.

McDougall, J. (1974). The anonymous spectator—*A clinical study of sexual perversion. Contemporary Psychoanalysis, 10*: 289–310.

McDougall, J. (1986). Eve's reflection: on the homosexual components of female sexuality. In: H. Meyers (Ed.), *Between Analyst and Patient* (pp. 213–228). Hillsdale, NJ: Analytic Press.

McDougall, J. (1989a). The dead father: On early psychic trauma and its relation to disturbance in sexual identity and in creative activity. *International Journal Psycho-Analysis, 70*: 205–219.

McDougall, J. (1989b). *Theaters of the Body: A Psychoanalytic Approach to Psychosomatic Illness*. New York, USA: W. W. Norton & Company.

Milrod, D. (1990). The ego ideal. *The Psychoanalytic Study of the Child, 45*: 43–60.

Milrod, D. (2002). The superego. *The Psychoanalytic Study of the Child, 57*: 131–148.

Moncayo, R. (2006). The partial object, the ideal ego, the ego-ideal, and the empty subject. *The Psychoanalytic Review, 93*: 565–602.

Nietzsche, F. (1974). *The Gay Science*. New York: Vintage Books. (Original work published in 1882, 1887).

Nietzsche, F. (1982a). Twilight of the idols. In: W. Kaufmann (Ed.), *The Portable Nietzsche* (pp. 464–564). New York: Penguin Books (Originally published in 1888).

Nietzsche, F. (1982b). The antichirst. In: W. Kaufmann (Ed.), *The Portable Nietzsche* (pp. 569–656). New York: Penguin Books (Originally published in 1888).

Nietzsche, F. (1997). *Daybreak: Thoughts on the Prejudices of Morality*. Cambridge: Cambridge University Press (Originally published in 1881).

Nietzsche, F. (2000). Beyond good and evil. In: W. Kaufmann (Ed. and Trans.) *Basic Writings of Nietzsche* (pp. 179–436). USA: Modern Library (Originally published in 1886).

Ortega y Gasset, J. (1930). *The Revolt of the Masses*. New York: Norton, 1932.

Padel, J. (1991). Fairbairn's thought on the relationship of inner and outer worlds. Free Associations, 2D: 589–615.

Paskauskas, R. A. (1993). *The Complete Correspondence of Sigmund Freud and Ernest Jones 1908–1939*. Cambridge, MA/London: The Belknap Press of Harvard University Press.

Reich, A. (1954). Early identifications as archaic elements in the superego. *Journal of American Psychoanalysis Association, 2*: 218–238.

Reich, A. (1960). Pathologic forms of self-esteem regulation. *The Psychoanalytic Study of the Child, 15*: 215–232.

Reich, W. (1972). *SEX-POL: Essays 1929–1934*. New York, USA: Vintage Books.

Reich, W. (1973a). *Cancer Biopathy; Volme II of the Discovery of the Orgone*. New York, USA: Farrar, Straus and Giroux (originally published in 1943).

Reich, W. (1973b). *Ether, God and Devil and Cosmic Superimposition*. New York: Farrar, Straus and Giroux.

Reich, W. (1983). *Children of the Future*. Toronto, Canada: McGraw-Hill Ryerson.

Reich, W. (1990). *Character Analysis*. New York: Farrar, Straus and Giroux (Originally published in 1933).

Reik, T. (1963). *The Need to be Loved*. New York: The Noonday Press.

Róheim, G. (1941). The psycho-analytic interpretation of culture. *International Journal Psycho-Analysis, 22*: 147–169.

Rubin, G. (1975). The traffic in women: Notes on the "Political economy" of sex. In: R. Reiter (Ed.), *Toward an Anthropology of Women* (pp. 157–210.). New York, USA: Monthly Review Press.

Sachs, H. (1929). One of the motive factors in the formation on the superego in women. *International Journal Psycho-Analysis, 10*: 39–50.

Sagan, E. (1989). *Freud, Women, Morality*. USA: Basic Books.

Silver, J. (Producer), & A. Wachowski & L. Wachowski (Directors). (1999). *The Matrix*. [Motion Picture]. United States of America: Warner Bros. Pictures.

Spotnitz, H. (1969). *Modern Psychoanalysis of the Schizophrenic Patient*. New York, USA: Grune & Stratton.

Tausk, V. (1933). On the origin of the "Influencing machine" in Schizophrenia. *Psychoanalysis Quarterly, 2*: 519–556.

Tustin, F. (1984). Autistic Shapes. *International Review Psycho-Analysis, 11*: 279–290.

Tustin, F. (1988). The "black hole". *Free Associations, 1*: 35–50.

Van Ophuijsen, J. H. (1929). The sexual aim of sadism as manifested in acts of violence. *Interational Journal Psycho-Analysis, 10*: 139–144.

Vanggaard, T. (1972). *Phallos. A Symbol and its History in the Male World.* New York, USA: International Universities Press.

Winnicott, D. W. (1953). Transitional objects and transitional phenomena—A study of the first not-me possession. *International Journal Psycho-Analysis, 34*: 89–97.

Wittgenstein, L. (1969). *On Certainty.* Great Britain: Basil Blackwell Publishing.

Wittgenstein, L. (1970). *Zettel.* Los Angeles, USA: University of California Press, 1967.

Wittgenstein, L. (1983). *Remarks on the Foundation of Mathematics.* Great Britain: Basil Blackwell Publishing.

Wittgenstein, L (1991). *Remarks on the Philosophy of Psychology.* Oxford, UK: Blackwell Publishing Ltd., 1980.

Wittgenstein, L. (2001). *Philosophical Investigations.* Malden, MA: Blackwell Publishing, 1953.

Wurmser, L. (1988). "The sleeping giant": A dissenting comment about "Borderline Pathology". *Psychoanalytic Inquiry, 8*: 373–397.

Wurmser, L. (2003). The annihilating power of absoluteness. *Psychoanalytic Psychology, 20*: 214–235.

Žižek, S. (2006). *How to Read Lacan.* New York: W. W. Norton Company.

INDEX